BRICKLAYING
SIMPLIFIED

OUTDOOR BARBECUES

DONALD R. BRANN

Library of Congress Card No. 77-140968

FIFTH PRINTING — 1976
REVISED EDITION

Published by
DIRECTIONS SIMPLIFIED, INC.

Division of
EASI-BILD PATTERN CO., INC.
Briarcliff Manor, NY 10510

FIRST PRINTING
© 1971

REVISED EDITIONS
1972,1973,1975,1976

NOTE
Due to the variance in quality and availability of many materials and
products, always follow directions a manufacturer and/or retailer offers.
Unless products are used exactly as the manufacturer specifies, its war-
ranty can be voided. While the author mentions certain products by trade
name, no endorsement or end use guarantee is implied. In every case the
author suggests end uses as specified by the manufacturer prior to
publication.

Since manufacturers frequently change ingredients or formula and/or
introduce new and improved products, or fail to distribute in certain
areas, trade names are mentioned to help the reader zero in on products
of comparable quality and end use.   The Publisher

IT'S EASY WHEN YOU KNOW HOW

Anyone who can learn to cook, sew, or saw a board following a drawn line,can learn to lay bricks. And like hand-sewing that requires uniform stitches, or cooking that requires proper seasoning, bricklaying requires a properly prepared mortar mix, plus uniform mortar joints. The first few bricks you lay will prove to be the most difficult, but like making love, bricklaying is something everyone can do by instinct, enjoy doing while learning, and become real good with practice. But first read through this book and note each illustration everytime it's mentioned. While some are referred to several times, note how each step relates to the one previously mentioned. And always refer to the text when you attempt doing any job the first time.

Mixing and spreading mortar, picking up and placing brick, flexes muscles while it stimulates the blood. The mind, completely engrossed in a new activity, is like a motor idling in neutral. Hours speed by and when a day's work is done, it is sometimes hard to remember what was bugging you when you started.

Don't sell yourself short. As each of us makes a pass at learning to live, we tend to rate our capabilities according to past results. If we were all thumbs in a grammar or junior high manual training class, we frequently go through many adult years thinking we are equally inept. Few adults even test themselves to see if a hammer or a saw is still hard to handle. Don't let this happen to you.

Learning any skill or profession starts with words, pictures, instruction and participation. Learning to lay bricks or blocks requires the same procedure. The sidewalk spectator who watches the bricklayer at work can learn much by watching. Bricklaying is one skill that can be self-taught during the time it takes to read through this book. To become proficient — requires practice.

TABLE OF CONTENTS

PREFACE TO PRACTICE

There are many preliminary steps that must be taken before starting to lay bricks. These include selecting the exact site, laying out guidelines, excavating, grading, erecting forms for footings where same are required, pouring footings, setting up guide lines or corner poles, mixing mortar, etc.

While a brick walk or terrace can be laid on sand, over undisturbed soil, with no concrete slab required, building a form may seem like a lot of unnecessary work. Since a form automatically establishes an exact height above grade, plus an easy to follow guide that ensures sloping the walk or terrace to pitch drainage requires, it's worth the effort.

Many manufacturers produce brick measuring 2¼″ high, 3¾″ wide, 8″ long, Illus. 1. The industry also produces a "modular" size brick that measures 3⅝″ wide, 2¼″ high, 7⅝″ long. Non–Modular size brick is shown on chart below.

Unit Designation	Manufactured Size, in.		
	t	h	l
Three-inch	3	2-5/8	9-5/8
	3	2-3/4	9-3/4
Standard	3-3/4	2-1/4	8
Oversize	3-3/4	2-3/4	8

Illus. 1, describes position in which a brick is used.

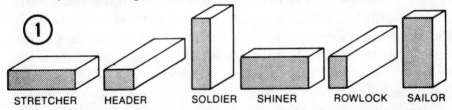

STRETCHER   HEADER   SOLDIER SHINER   ROWLOCK SAILOR

Always measure brick you buy and plan your work according to it's size. The three grades of brick of interest to most homeowners are designated SW (severe weathering), MW (medium weathering), NW (no weathering). SW and MW brick may be used in walls exposed to weather. NW should be used only in interior work.

MAKE A DRY RUN

First practice laying a course of brick dry up to a line or straight edge, Illus. 2, Space bricks ⅜" or ½" apart. Use a scrap of plywood as a gauge, Illus. 3, or your index finger.

While you never start laying brick until you have laid the necessary footings, during preliminary practice sessions, use a 2x4 in place of a concrete footing. Spread mortar and bed brick No. 1 and 2 against a straight edge, Illus. 2. Leave other bricks in position. Now check brick No. 1 and No. 2 with a level. Stretch a line between brick No. 1 and 2. Wrap line around another brick at each end. Carefully position line along the near edge of bricks 1 and 2, Illus. 15. Lay other bricks to the line, without touching line. Always lay bricks to a line. Always check with a level.

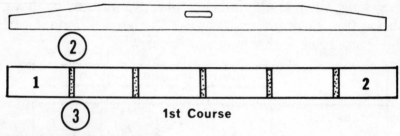

1st Course

BRICK MORTAR MIX

The strength of a brick wall and it's resistance to penetration of rain and cold depends to a great degree on the mortar and the bond it develops. Water in mortar is essential to the bond and if the mortar has insufficient water, the bond will be weak and spotty. While concrete must be mixed with a limited amount of water, mortar should be mixed with the maximum amount of water it's possible to use, and still produce a workable mortar. Note mortar shown in Illus. 26. It's plastic, easy to work, holds it's shape when in place or pressed out of a joint, Illus. 39, and permits being cut away.

If, after mixing, the mortar stiffens, due to the heat of day or normal evaporation, additional water should be added and the mortar remixed. This is called retempering and should always be done when the need arises. Always use up a batch of mortar

within 2½ hours after mixing. Equally important is the need to continually "work" the mix. Keep turning it over with your trowel every time you reach for a trowel full, to keep it awake and alive.

Properly mixed mortar will spread with little effort and still adhere to vertical surfaces. Never tap or attempt to move a brick after mortar has begun to harden. This breaks the bond and the mortar will no longer re-adhere to the brick. Always allow mortar to dry cure. While it's better to cure concrete by wetting, brick mortar should never be sprayed.

One of the most common defects in mixing mortar is oversanding. This is most likely to occur when you try to mix mortar using a shovel as a measure. For large jobs use the bottomless measuring box, Illus. 57. For small jobs buy prepared mortar mix, or buy a plastic or metal bucket with straight sides so you can accurately measure any portion needed. Good mortar necessitates using clean fine sand completely free of silt, clay, loam or pebbles.

Accurately measure sand and spread it over bottom of mixing tub. Accurately measure cement and mix the sand with cement until you get one overall color. Next measure and add lime and mix it until you again have achieved a complete mix. Always use a masonry hoe, and mix each thoroughly before adding the next ingredient. Mix all thoroughly before adding water.

For your first few practice bricklaying sessions, buy prepared mortar mixes. These only require adding water in exact proportion directions on bag recommend. Dump the contents into a mixing tub or wheelbarrow, spread it out and make a pocket. Add as much water as specified. Use the hoe to pull the dry mix into the water.

If local codes specify type M, S, N or O mortar, here is what they refer to.

Type M — 1 part Portland cement, ¼ part hydrated lime and not less than 2¼ or more than 3 parts sand by volume. This is a high strength mortar and is suitable for reinforced brick masonry, or other masonry below grade that is in contact with the earth, such as foundations, retaining walls, walks, sewers, manholes, catch basins.

Type S — 1 part Portland cement, ½ part hydrated lime and not less than 3½ or more than 4½ parts of sand by volume.

Type N — 1 part Portland cement, 1 part hydrated lime and not less than 4½ or more than 6 parts sand by volume. This mortar is considered a medium strength mortar and is recommended for exposed masonry above grade, walls, chimneys, and exterior brick work subject to severe exposure.

Type O — 1 part Portland cement, 2 parts hydrated lime and not less than 6¾ or more than 9 parts of sand. This mortar is suitable for non load-bearing walls.

CONCRETE FOR FOOTINGS

A 1-3-5 mix is acceptable for most footings. This means 1 bag (1 cubic foot of cement) to 3 cubic feet of sand to 5 cubic feet of gravel. For small jobs buy prepared mixes. While they cost a little more, they are great time savers. When you lay a large footing buy ready mix. If this isn't convenient, rent a small concrete mixer.

METAL CLIP

④

Metal clips placed 16" apart permit nailing studs to wall.

The SCR brick, Illus. 4, measures 5½″ by 2¼″ by 11½″*. This is acceptable by most building codes for 1 story load bearing walls.

* Actual size

Nominal Modular Sizes of Brick

Unit Designation	Thickness, in.	Face Dimension	
		Height, in.	Length, in.
Modular brick	4	2 2/3	8
Roman brick	4	2	12
Norman brick	4	2 2/3	12
Engineer's brick	4	3 1/5	8
Economy brick	4	4	8
King Norman brick	4	4	12
Double brick	4	5 1/3	8
Triple brick	4	5 1/3	12
"SCR brick" **	6	2 2/3	12

** With mortar

⑤

⑥

2½″

9″

4½″

Illus. 5, lists other kinds of brick. Each was designed for specific end uses.

Many homeowners will have need for one additional kind, fire brick, Illus. 6. Standard fire brick measures 9″ x 4½″ x 2½″. These are usually laid (9″ x 4½″) on the hearth, back wall and flared sides of a fireplace.

Always lay fire brick with a minimum size joint. Always use refractory air setting high temperature cement mortar. This comes wet, in cans. You need approximately four fire brick for each square foot when laid with a 9 x 4½" face exposed.

Seven bricks cover one square foot when the 9 x 2½" face is exposed. Approximately 35 lbs. of mortar is needed for each 100 fire brick when laid with a minimum size joint.

Laying brick requires placing each in position the first course determines, then overlapping joints on each course. Bricks laid the length of the wall, in position shown, Illus. 7, are called stretchers.

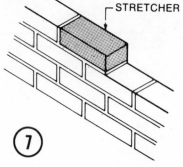

STRETCHER

⑦

A 4" thick stretcher wall, Illus. 8, makes an excellent fence or privacy partition.

⑧

Brick facing on a house is laid up the same way. The only difference is in the use of 22 gauge corrugated metal ties, Illus. 9. These are embedded in mortar and nailed to studs in wall every 24 inches horizontally and vertically, Illus. 10. This provides one tie for every 4 square feet of wall area or as specified in Illus. 11.

⑨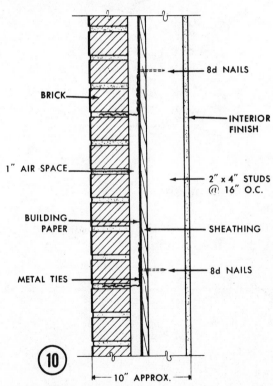

Bend and nail ties to studs with 8 penny nails. Embed ties in mortar bed in position shown, Illus. 10.

- 8d NAILS
- BRICK
- INTERIOR FINISH
- 1″ AIR SPACE
- 2″ x 4″ STUDS @ 16″ O.C.
- BUILDING PAPER
- SHEATHING
- METAL TIES
- 8d NAILS

⑩

← 10″ APPROX. →

Illus. 11, specifies placement of metal ties recommended in high wind areas.

Brick Veneer Tie Spacing

	Design Wind Load, psf	Spacing Horizontal by Vertical, in.	Wall Area per Tie, sq ft
⑪	20	24 by 24	4
	30	16 by 24	2 2/3
	40	16 by 18	2

You will need approximately 5.5 cubic feet of mortar for each 100 square feet of wall when laid with a ⅜″ joint; 7.0 cubic feet for ½″ joints. You will need approximately 675 bricks for 100 square feet. Add 5% for breakage.

A 4″ free-standing stretcher wall, Illus. 12, must be reinforced with pilasters. The pilaster is locked into the wall with headers in each course.

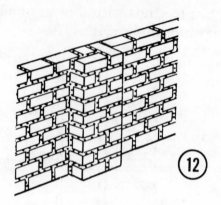

Illus. 13 shows the first course.

Illus. 14 the second course. Complete details for building a 4″ privacy wall are described on page 53.

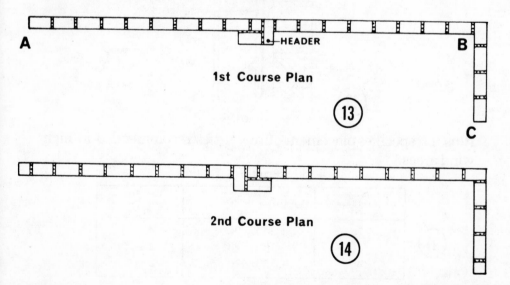

A

•—HEADER

B

1st Course Plan

⑬

C

2nd Course Plan

⑭

THE BASICS OF BRICKLAYING

Bricklaying only begins after you know how to select a site, build necessary forms, lay footings and foundation, have learned what tools to use, etc. Simply stated, bricklaying requires mixing mortar properly and spreading it over a limited area so it doesn't dry out before bricks are bedded. It's necessary to apply plenty of mortar to the end of each brick, and to keep all head and bed joints, Illus. 22, equal; to install flashing and provide weep holes for drainage where specified.

If you shove each brick into position and allow the mortar to squeeze out at the top of the head joint, you make a good joint.

Always butter up ends and sides of all closure bricks to make certain mortar squeezes out of the bed, as well as the head joint. Always apply parging, Illus. 45, to the back side of face brick before backup units are laid. This prevents penetration of moisture. If a cavity wall is to be grouted, Illus. 24, no parging is required.

Properly tool all exposed mortar joints, page 31, when mortar is thumb print hard.

Carefully position line along the edge of bricks, Illus. 15.

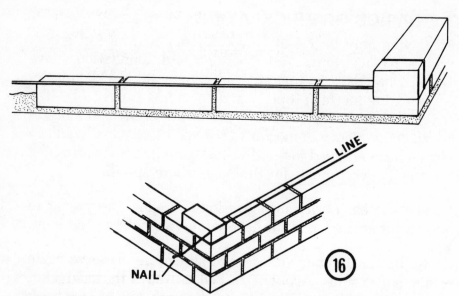

NAIL

LINE

(16)

A line holder, Illus. 17 simplifies running a line. A pair sells for less than a dollar. Makes an excellent gift for every homeowner. The line wraps around stem, goes through slot in fork, then through groove between brick and flat surface. Tension on line holds line holders in position.

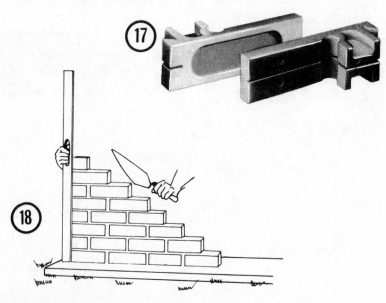

(17)

(18)

Most pros build up the corners first, Illus. 18; using a level to check each course level and plumb.

If you plan on doing a big job, do as the pros do — erect corner poles, Illus. 19. These can be purchased, rented, or made from readily available components, as explained on page 42. Corner poles save considerable time and help establish the exact thickness of each mortar joint. When plumbed in position, and the first course set at height required, the line can be moved up the pole to notches or marks that indicate height of each course.

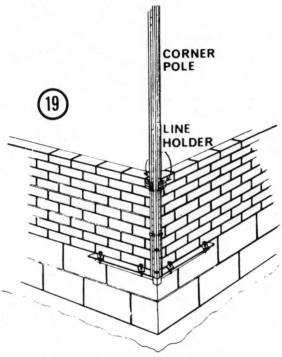

CORNER POLE

LINE HOLDER

Always keep the guide line taut. If it sags, it's valueless. On long walls a line will need to be supported at various intervals to keep it in alignment. Intermediate line supporters are called line pins or "trigs," Illus. 20. These are usually needed every 8 feet. To position a trig, place a brick on a small piece of plywood, equal in thickness to a bed joint. Place trig in position. Hold trig with a brick.

To efficiently lay bricks to a line requires spreading mortar without touching the line. Nor should fingers or brick touch the line. This requires coordination one quickly gains with practice. By positioning and releasing the brick at just the right moment, it can be pressed into position about $\frac{1}{16}''$ away from the line. The top edge of the brick must be pressed level to the line while the bottom edge is in line with the course below. Always avoid "crowding the line." Crowding could cause a bulge in the wall.

The end bricks No. 1 and No. 2, Illus. 3, establish the height of the first course. Always level a course using the end bricks as your guide. Always check each course to make certain it's straight (to the line), level, and plumb with other courses.

To lay up the second course, Illus. 21, start with a half-brick at ends, lay bricks No. 3 and 4, then set your guide line. The third course will contain bricks in position shown in the first course, Illus. 3, while the fourth course duplicates position of bricks laid out for the second course.

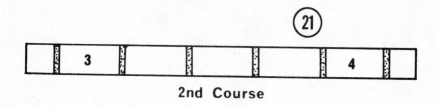

2nd Course

The bed and head joints, Illus. 22, should always be the same thickness. This can be $\frac{3}{8}''$ or $\frac{1}{2}''$.

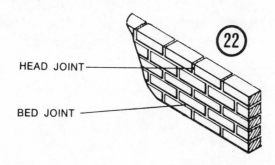

HEAD JOINT

BED JOINT

When laying up a double tiered or cavity wall, Illus. 23, always bevel the bed joint. This eliminates any excess mortar from protruding beyond the edge. Always use the kind of steel reinforcing suggested, and space it in position specified, Illus. 24.

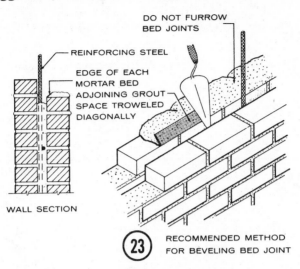

DO NOT FURROW
BED JOINTS

REINFORCING STEEL

EDGE OF EACH
MORTAR BED
ADJOINING GROUT
SPACE TROWELED
DIAGONALLY

WALL SECTION

(23) RECOMMENDED METHOD
FOR BEVELING BED JOINT

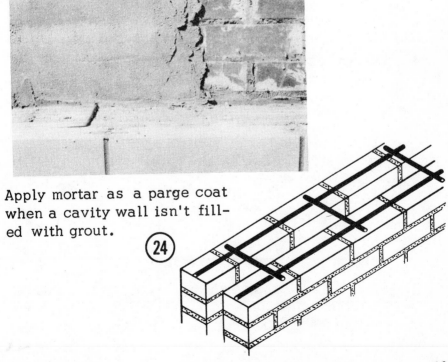

Apply mortar as a parge coat when a cavity wall isn't filled with grout.

(24)

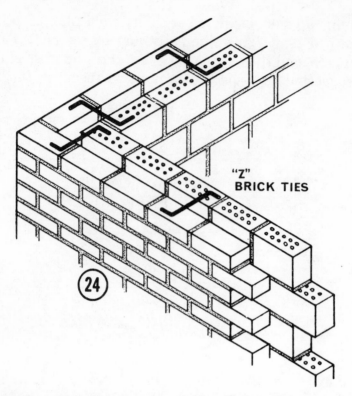

"Z"
BRICK TIES

(24)

Head joints, Illus. 25, should be full. The best joints are formed by shoving the brick into place. Shoved joints produce a solid wall section leaving no cavity in which water can collect. If you have trouble sticking mortar on head of brick, do this. Press end of brick into mortar on board, before applying mortar to head.

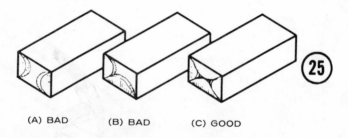

(A) BAD   (B) BAD   (C) GOOD   (25)

Molded brick are always laid with the trade mark face down. Bricks are still manufactured in some areas with a square edge on one side and a slight bevel on the other. Always place the square edge out.

TO CUT BRICK

Draw a line to indicate cut. Place brick on a level spot. Even better, on a bag of sand, **Illus. 29.** Using a blocking chisel and a hammer, Illus. 28, strike chisel. Always face beveled edge of chisel towards part of brick you don't want to use. When a cut brick is used on an exposed end, always place uncut end out. You can also cut brick with the cutting end of a brick hammer. Practice cutting, and you will be surprised to see how quickly you can become **proficient, Illus. 27.**

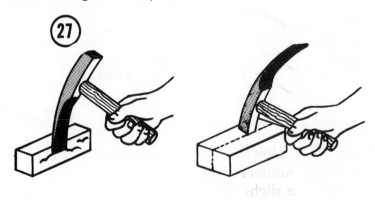

Cutting a brick to one-half or three-quarter size or to angle needed, isn't difficult. Use a bevel square, Illus. 55. Draw a line across brick and use a blocking chisel and hammer to cut brick.

Placing a brick on a sandbag, then cutting with a chisel or hammer simplifies making clean cuts, Illus. 29. A cut brick is called a bat.

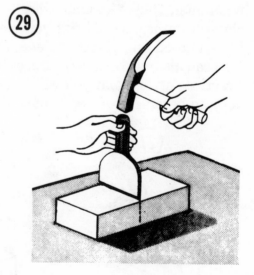

BRICK CUTTER
A solid whack with a
2-lb. hammer (or heavier)
cuts brick to size or
angle required. This is
a good item to rent.

LEARN THE NAMES

Bricks laid in position shown, Illus. 13, 30, are called headers.

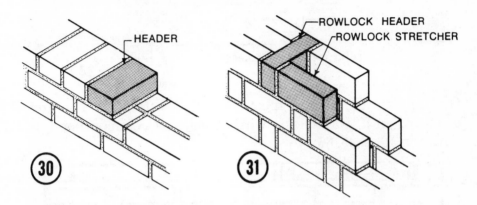

Bricks laid on edge, Illus. 31, are called a rowlock; rowlock header, or a rowlock stretcher. Rowlocks are usually placed under a window or door frame. Use a rowlock course to start a wall, or use a course to gain additional height.

A single course of brick, Illus. 32, is called a wythe or tier.

A soldier course is shown in Illus. 33, a sailor in Illus. 1.

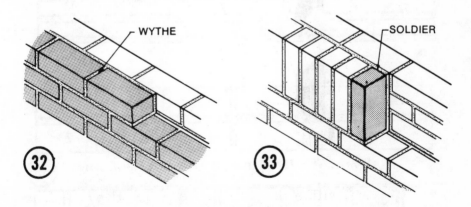

If you are laying a brick walk or terrace, the edge brick could be sailors or soldiers. The sailor edging shown in Illus. 34, is embedded in concrete. Complete instructions for laying a brick walk are explained on page 78.

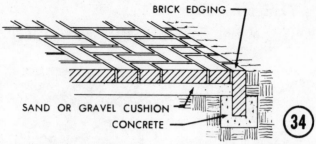

BRICK EDGING

SAND OR GRAVEL CUSHION

CONCRETE

(34)

Overlapping joints on each course provides strength. The first course of an 8″ wall laid in what is called a common bond, is shown in Illus. 35, 36.

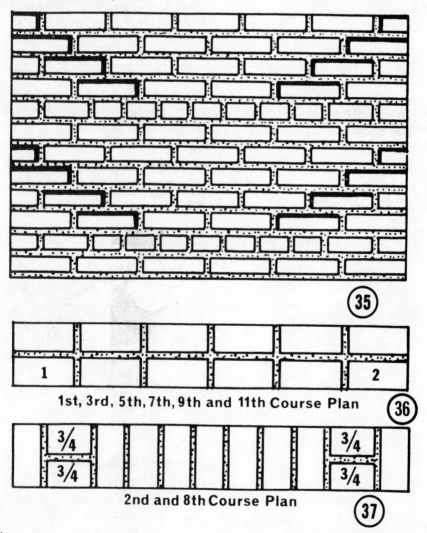

(35)

1   2

1st, 3rd, 5th, 7th, 9th and 11th Course Plan   (36)

3/4   3/4

3/4   3/4

2nd and 8th Course Plan   (37)

The second course is shown in Illus. 37. The first course would be duplicated for the third, fifth, seventh, ninth and eleventh courses.

The fourth course, Illus. 38, would also be laid for the sixth, tenth, and twelfth courses. The second course, Illus. 37, would be duplicated for the eighth course.

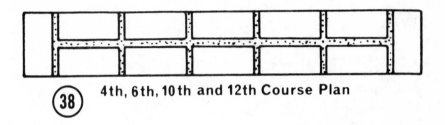

38   **4th, 6th, 10th and 12th Course Plan**

Always cut surplus mortar away from joint, Illus. 39. Throw it back into the mortar on board. Before taking another full trowel, work the glob thrown back into the mortar so it doesn't become a dry, hardened orphan. Always cut away mortar as quickly as it is squeezed out. This prevents staining face of brick.

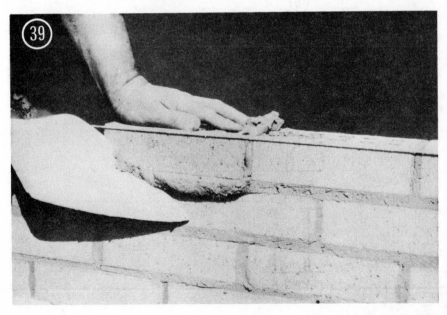

When laying up two or more tiers, practice laying brick by beveling the mortar, Illus. 40. The object is to lay mortar so the finished bed and head joints are full and of uniform thickness, and none protrudes into cavity; and to use metal ties and/or reinforcing specified.

BEVELING BED JOINTS

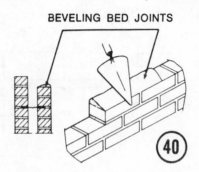

Always butter up the head of each brick, or a side of a rowlock, Illus. 41, before placing in position. Partially filled mortar joints result in leaky walls, reduce the strength of masonry, and contribute to cracking, due to water penetration, freezing and thawing.

Always butter up both ends of a closure brick, Illus. 42, before placing in position.

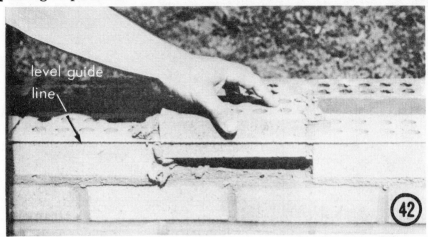

When laying up an 8″ or thicker wall, or any cavity wall, Illus. 43, don't allow any mortar to fall into cavity. Beveling the bed prevents this, but if you are working fast, or have an inexperienced helper laying up the back tier, hang a 1x2, or strip of lumber, Illus. 44, cut to width cavity allows, between tiers. Using wire, hang this strip just below course you are working on. This catches all droppings.

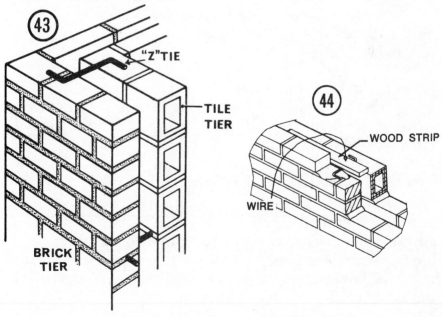

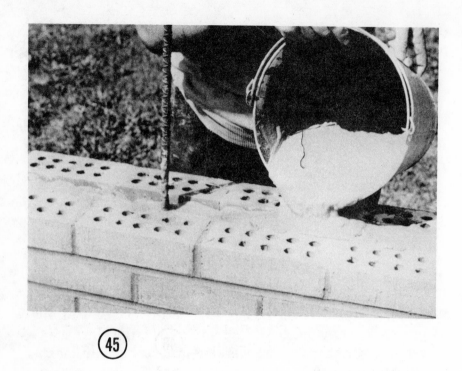

(45)

Unless the cavity is kept clean, you will have difficulty filling the void with grout, Illus. 45. The cavity wall must be kept clean at all times. This is especially important when building a reinforced brick wall. Unless you keep cavity free, the grout won't have a chance to fill all joints, crevices and bond reinforcing rods to brick.

Grout is mortar that's almost fluid. This permits grout to fill all joints, adhere completely to reinforcing ties, and bond both tiers together. While good mortar will stick to the bottom of a trowel, grout will slide off.

FINISHING MORTAR JOINTS

Always finish the joint, Illus. 46, with a steel jointer or trowel, as soon as the mortar becomes thumbprint hard. You can usually lay 3, 4 or 5 eight foot courses of brick before mortar permits use of jointer. The Concave or V joint provides greatest resistance to the weather. Use jointer slightly larger than mortar joint.

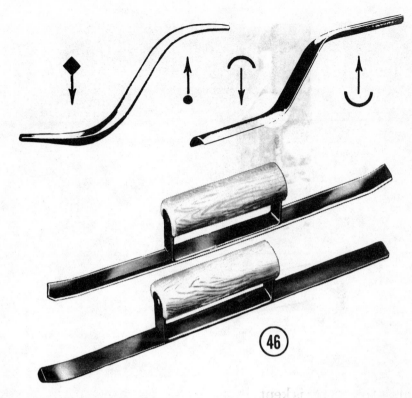

Illus. 47 shows various mortar joints you can finish. A troweled joint, (3, 4, 5) is one where the mortar is cut off with the trowel and finished with the trowel, Illus. 48.

The weathered joint, Illus. 47-3, must be worked from below course using a trowel.

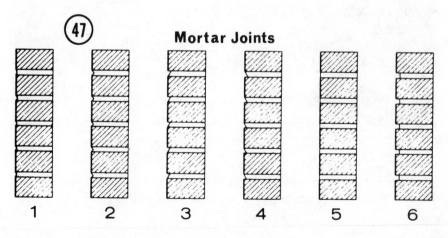

Mortar Joints

1   2   3   4   5   6

48

A concave joint, Illus. 49, or V shaped joint, Illus. 50, are recommended in areas where there is a lot of rain.

(49) **Concave Jointer**

(50) **V Jointer**

Jointers, Illus. 46, are available with a V joint at one end that tapers from ⅜" to ³⁄₁₆"; and a round end that tapers from ½" to ³⁄₁₆". Or you can buy a concave jointer, that has ⅜" on one end, ½" on the other; or ⅝" and ¾".

As noted, mortar joints can be troweled or tooled. In the troweled joint, the excess mortar is simply cut off (struck) with a trowel and finished with a trowel. This can be a rough cut or flush joint, Illus. 47(5), 48.

City brownstones, four and five story houses that formerly housed the wealthy, were usually built with brick. Since the walls were originally covered with lathe and plaster, the mortar joints were struck, Illus. 48. When the cracked plaster is removed, the exposed brick makes a handsome wall.

Never "slush" the joints. This refers to filling in after brick is placed. It's much better to apply a thick slab to the head of a brick, then cut it away.

Never start to mix mortar until you are ready to lay brick. Always check guide lines to make certain they are level. If you use corner poles these must be checked to make certain they are plumb and in correct position. Pile brick within convenient reach but don't clutter up your working area.

BENCHMARK

Watch an experienced bricklayer set up a job and you see him make a mark on a post, pier, wall or column. This one mark will be referred to when estimating number of courses, and thickness of mortar joint needed to lay courses up to a door or window opening. He will set the first course for the corner poles from this mark. He will also refer to this mark when he uses a story pole. This point is called a BENCHMARK.

TOOLS REQUIRED

Just as you wouldn't think of learning to play golf until you bought, rented or borrowed a set of clubs, so must you buy or rent all the tools needed for masonry work. These consist of a mixing tub, measuring box, shovel, hoe, trowels, brick hammer, blocking chisel, 6 foot spacing rule, plus a 4 foot level, which masons call a plumb rule. You will also need a line, line level, gage stick, and for many jobs a scaffold. Corner poles and/or line holders are optional, Illus. 51.

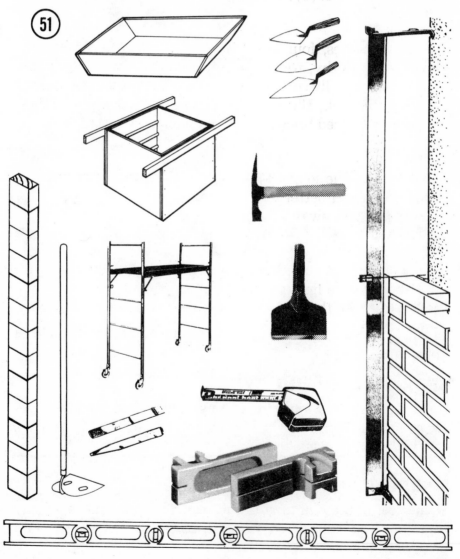

An investment in tools is sound since you can usually recoup its cost on your first job. One company offers an apprentice's bricklayers' tool kit, Illus. 52, that contains the hand tools needed. It contains a practical assortment including a 6 foot spacing rule, 48" mahogany level, an 11" trowel, a 5½" pointing trowel, brick hammer, 3" brick chisel, one ⅜x½", and one ⅝x¾" jointer, a 250 foot line, one pair of corner blocks. This kit makes a perfect gift for the man who has everything — but peace of mind.

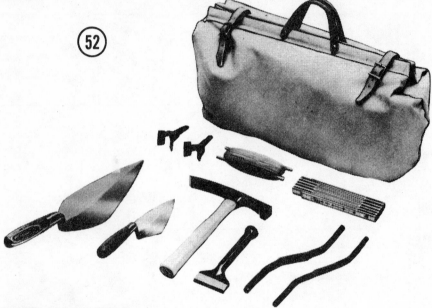

LINE HOLDERS

Illus. 17, described previously, provide one way to establish level guide lines.

SPRING STEEL LINE TWIGS

Illus. 20, support a long line from sagging when stretched between line holders. Four inch in length, five-eighths wide, trigs cost little but do a lot.

MIXING TUB

If the cost of a metal mixing tub seems like an expensive way to get started, consider renting or making one. Directions on page 40 explain how.

BRICK TROWEL

The brick trowel is one of the three most important tools in laying brick. The way you use, or misuse it, is important for several reasons. If you select a trowel that is too big, your wrist muscles tire fast and you'll begin to think bricklaying is not for you. Handle each size trowel and select the one that feels good. Use the same thought in selecting a trowel as you would in selecting a golf club or tennis racquet.

While a small trowel will, in the beginning, slow you down, it's better to do less than wear yourself out fast. Remember, brick laying requires a combination of muscle and body movement you probably haven't used before. So start slow, don't expect too much too fast, and remember, like golf or tennis, the beginning always looks bleak.

A short wide trowel is recommended since it places the weight of mortar closer to your wrist. As you develop rhythm, and become acclimated to the work, your ability to pick up and spread the mortar properly will improve. At this time, switch to a larger trowel.

SIX FOOT FOLDING RULE

A six foot folding rule having a brick course scale printed on one side, is very handy. These locate various size mortar joints. Study this rule and you begin to see how it simplifies laying each course to exact height a door, window, arch or other opening requires. The rule shows 4 courses to 10½", a 2¼" brick plus ⅜" mortar measures 2⅝". The rule indicates this as No. 4. The second course will be laid at 5¼". This is also clearly marked with a 4. Each course using the ⅜" joint is numbered 4. This is called a 10½" gauge, Illus. 53, 54.

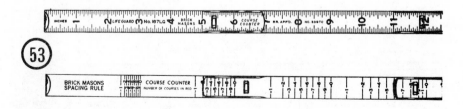

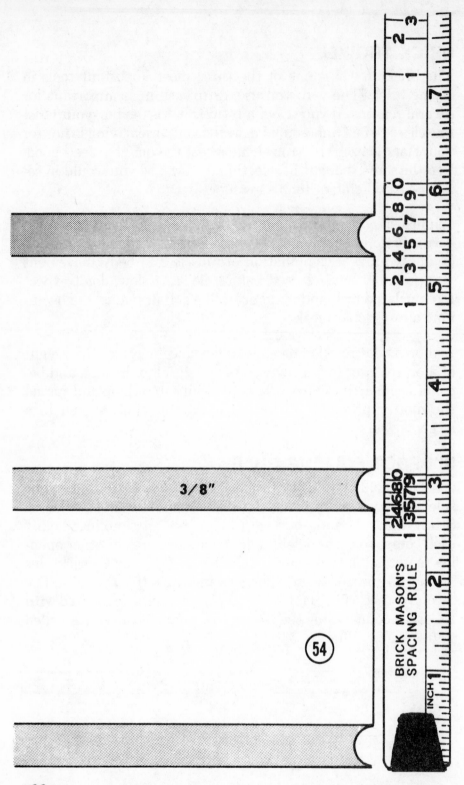

3/8"

(54)

BRICK MASON'S
SPACING RULE

The rule also shows 4 courses to 11″. This requires a ½″ mortar joint. The first course is 2¾″ and is identified by 6. The second course at 5½″ is also marked 6 as are subsequent courses. This is called an 11″ gauge and is identified with the No. 6. Use this rule if you want to lay out and make corner poles, a story pole, or a gage stick.

CARPENTERS AND BEVEL SQUARE

Illus. 55. The large carpenter square helps lay out guidelines and check corners during construction. A bevel square helps establish exact angle to cut brick.

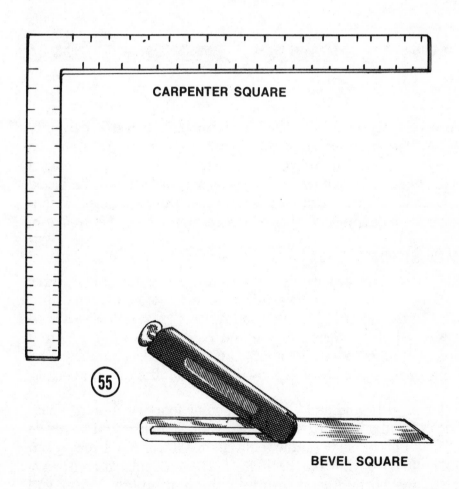

CARPENTER SQUARE

55

BEVEL SQUARE

BLOCKING CHISEL

The blocking chisel permits cutting brick to size and shape required. Chisel has a beveled cutting edge and a straight back. Keep beveled edge towards you, flat face against piece of brick you want to use, Illus. 29.

LEVEL

Illus. 56. The level is a vitally important tool. Bricklayers call these a plumb rule. Available in hardwood, aluminum and other light metals, two are needed — one 42" or 48", the other 12". Both are continually used to check work horizontally as well as vertically.

Since the accuracy of a level is all important, test it carefully before purchase to make certain it's 100% accurate, then use and treasure it. Don't drop, bang, or misuse it. Don't tap a level with the handle of a trowel or hammer in order to level a brick. Always clean the level carefully to keep any particles of concrete from bonding. Always oil it after use to keep it store fresh.

MEASURING BOX

To mix mortar accurately, you need to measure cement, lime, and sand. To simplify measuring, build a bottomless box, Illus. 57. Cut two pieces of ¾" plywood A — 13½x12, two pieces B — 12x12. Apply waterproof glue and nail A to B using 8 penny common nails spaced 3" apart. Cut two 1x2x24" handles. Nail handles to box in position shown. Rasp handles to round edges.

Fill box with sand and you have 1 cubic foot. To simplify measuring smaller quantities, nail strips of ⅜" half round to inside of box. For a quarter cubic foot nail one 3" from bottom; 6" up for half; 9" from bottom for three quarters of a cubic foot. Always place the bottomless measure in the mortar tub. When you have filled amount required, remove measure.

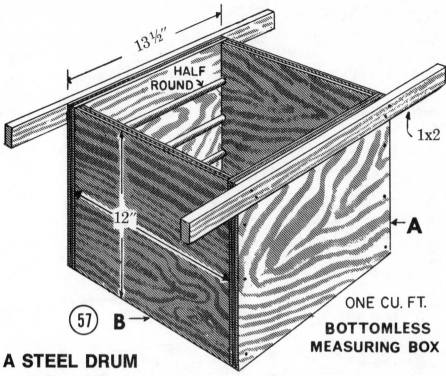

13½"

HALF ROUND

1x2

12"

← **A**

ONE CU. FT.

BOTTOMLESS MEASURING BOX

(57) **B** →

A STEEL DRUM

Half filled with water, provides a handy way to clean a hoe and shovel. A pail of water simplifies cleaning a trowel before any cement can start to dry. Always wash masonry tools after use. Keep tools store fresh. Don't hesitate to rub motor oil over the blade of a trowel, hoe and shovel before storing. Rust on a trowel prevents mortar from sliding freely.

Keep a couple of galvanized pails handy. Besides providing an instant supply of water needed to keep mortar alive, a wet pail provides a carrying bucket for mortar. Be sure to douse pail in water before filling with mortar. Always wash a pail out before mortar can harden.

MORTAR BOARD

You will also need a mortar board, Illus. 26. This can be ¾" plywood, 2'x2' or 30"x30" mounted on 2x4's or sawhorses. The mortar board must always be placed at a convenient height and within arms length of your working area. Always wet mortar board before dumping a pail of mortar.

MORTAR TUB

You can mix mortar in an oversized wheelbarrow or build a mortar tub, Illus. 58. Cut 2 sides A, 1x12 to angle shown. Cut 2 ends B, 1x12. Apply waterproof glue and nail sides to ends. Apply glue and nail a 3/16" tempered hardboard panel to bottom.

Always place mortar tub on a level surface. If you use it where it needs to be supported to make level, nail an extra 3/8" or 1/2" plywood panel to bottom as a stiffener.

Paint tub with wood preservative. When thoroughly dry, paint inside surface with used crankcase oil. After using, always scrape out concrete and hose tub thoroughly. When dry, paint with old crankcase oil before reusing.

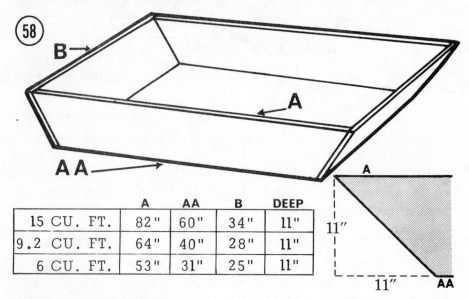

	A	AA	B	DEEP
15 CU. FT.	82"	60"	34"	11"
9.2 CU. FT.	64"	40"	28"	11"
6 CU. FT.	53"	31"	25"	11"

CORNER POLES

Watch an experienced bricklayer set up a job and after the footings are completed, he places corner poles, Illus. 19, 59, in position. The line for the first course is stretched between poles. To permit placing doors and windows at exact height desired, the bed for the first course may be slightly thicker to achieve exact height required or one or more Rowlock courses can be laid.

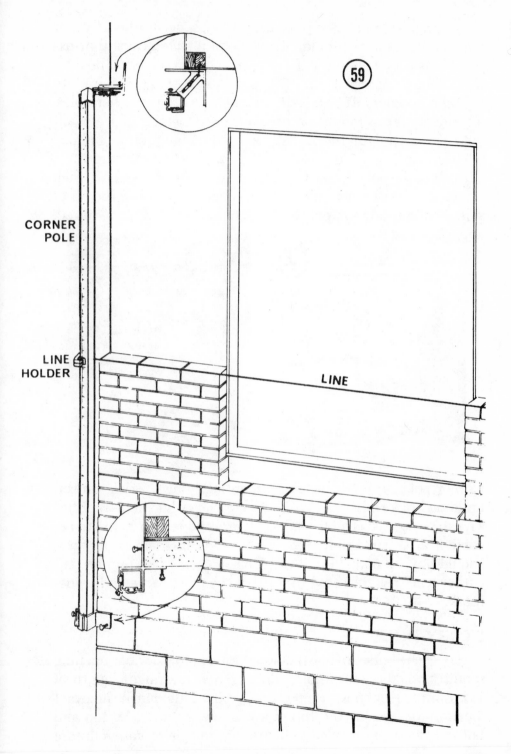

CORNER
POLE

LINE
HOLDER

LINE

59

Corner poles greatly simplify laying brick accurately. Corner pole manufacturers provide many helpful suggestions that explain how to erect and use. Be sure to ask for a direction booklet if you rent corner poles. Illus. 60 shows how corner poles simplify laying up corners. If you want to make your own corner poles, a complete set of mounting brackets and line guides are available. Use a straight 1x2, or 2x2, or 1" square aluminum tubing. Secure pole in plumb position, then tape a flat spacing tape, Illus. 61 to the pole. These tapes have easy to read standard brick course spacings on one side, modular block spacing on the other side. Position tape on pole so first course is at height required, and away you go.

Corner poles are indispensible when applying a brick veneer, building brick walls, etc. While two bricks or line holders, Illus. 17, can be used to establish a level line, anyone who wants to become a pro, or make money laying brick in their spare time, should buy, or make a pair of corner poles. If you buy or rent corner poles ask for those that carry the SCR name and trademark.

STORY POLE

To lay each course up to exact height a window or door opening requires, make a story pole, Illus. 62. Use a straight length of 1x2x6' or 8'. Fasten a spacing tape, on one side; mark the exact location for bottom and top of a window on one face; top and bottom of a door on an edge. The story pole helps you maintain the thickness of bed joints needed to lay up each course. Always place the story pole at a point level with your Benchmark.

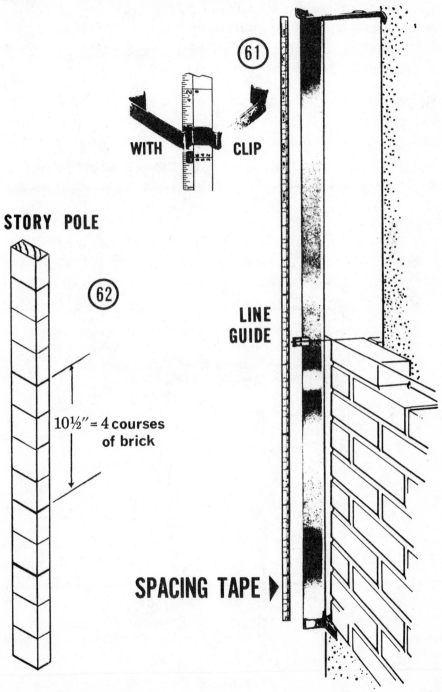

61 WITH CLIP

STORY POLE

62

10½" = 4 courses of brick

LINE GUIDE

SPACING TAPE ▶

GAGE STICK

A gage stick is a short story pole, usually 42″ to 48″ long. A bricklayer will lay out one side of a gage stick with ⅜″ mortar joints, another side with ½″ joints. By constantly checking with the gage stick he keeps courses to height required. A gage stick is a lot handier to use than a story pole.

SCAFFOLD

Bricklaying is one job that requires every tool the work requires. If you build a wall that requires lifting bricks higher than a comfortable height, erect a platform using 2x8 or 2x10 planks on one course of concrete blocks or sawhorses. Stack the bricks on the platform. If you are building a wall over 5 feet in height, or veneering the face of a building, a scaffold will be needed. These can be rented, Illus. 63, and are well worth the cost. This type adjusts from 16″ to 75″ and provides a 28″x75″ platform. One person can erect and move it.

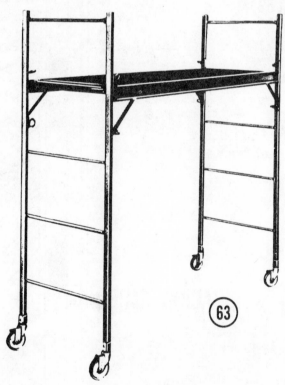

A scaffold must be rigid. Since it needs to support you, a mortar board, mortar and bricks, and must be moved continuously, rent a length you can handle.

An adjustable scaffold eliminates unnecessary bending and stooping and a considerable amount of fatigue. Don't rent or build a flimsy scaffold. Remember, it must provide solid support. Any movement in a scaffold is not only hazardous to you and anyone passing by, but also prevents laying brick accurately.

An easy to build scaffold is shown in Illus. 64. These "jiffy jacks" can be rented. 2x4 legs can be cut to length required. A screw locking bracket permits adjusting legs to any slope. Use 2x4, free of knots for legs. Brackets will accommodate legs from two to twelve feet in length.

2x6 or 2x8

JIFFY
JACKS

←2x4

64

65

If a scaffold is being erected on recently filled soil, place scaffold on 2x6 planks. Use 2x8 or 2x10 lumber free of knots for platform. Never allow planks to extend more than 12″ beyond end of saw-horses.

If you rent a rolling scaffold, always remove brick, mortar board, and tools from scaffold before moving. Always apply brakes to casters before climbing up on a caster mounted scaffold. Always anchor a scaffold to the building with guy ropes when a slope, high wind, etc., etc., necessitates same.

SITE SELECTION

Regardless of what job you plan, it's exact location and distance from property line is of prime importance. In most surburban areas it's necessary to obtain a permit to build any type of permanent structure. If you want to build a brick wall along your property line, make certain you dig foundation trenches and lay footings on, or at a distance from property line your survey and local codes require. Don't cut roots of your neighbors trees until you have consulted your insurance man as to liability.

Masonry construction requires a site where natural run-off of water will not be interrupted. Unless adequate drainage is provided, your best efforts will be destroyed if water collects and freezes, or rain undermines footings. It's also important not to create a runoff, or pool of water that may damage your neighbors property.

If you build on a steep slope that has an outcropping of rock, use reinforcing rods to lock footing to rock. This isn't nearly as difficult as it may seem. Rent an electric hammer. Drill holes eight to ten inches deep. Insert ½″ or ⅝″ steel reinforcing rods in rock. Bend rod into footing form. When you pour footing allow free flowing mortar to lock rod to rock.

Rocky land frequently provides a lot of good living space at low cost. When a retaining wall is constructed, the area filled, leveled and seeded, a steep slope surrounded by a brick wall can be transformed into a charming garden spot.

If a low-lying site is selected for a brick wall, dig test holes. A post hole digger and a strong back can reveal what's below — clay, gravel or other hardpan. Dig as deep as you may need to go for footings. If you hit a layer of clay, sand or gravel, this makes a good base: proper size footings will usually provide the support your masonry requires.

Always spare trees when selecting a site and don't build too close to a small tree. The years fly by and small shrubs grow surprisingly fast. If in doubt about the size a tree or bush will be when full grown, consult your local nurseryman.

Always save the topsoil. Pile it away from your site. This will come in handy when you finish construction.

IMPORTANT FACTS TO REMEMBER

Laying brick, like swinging a golf club or tennis racquet, requires a freedom of movement. You have to bend, lift, accurately space and place each brick to a line. One quickly develops a combination of body and arm movements, a rhythm that doesn't strain or waste energy.

Always place your mortar tub within arms length. Don't stretch to reach mortar, don't allow the mortar box to crowd you into an uncomfortable position.

Two important suggestions. One — only buy as many bags of cement or mortar mix as you can use during the period you plan on working. Always store it on planks, placed on blocks. Cover completely with polyethylene or tarpaulin to keep dampness from getting in. Two — never start when you are tired. Always stop work when you begin to feel fatigued.

Always protect masonry work under construction to prevent saturation during a heavy rainstorm. Purchase a roll of polyethylene. Use it to cover work whenever you leave it overnight, particularily during cold, rainy weather. Be sure to tie or weight the cover to keep it from blowing away.

Don't stack brick or other masonry materials on bare ground. Preferably on planks. Always cover when not being used. Don't allow masonry materials to absorb moisture or to freeze.

Since some brick have a high rate of absorption, any exposed brick will absorb a great amount of water if it is exposed to the weather. Never attempt to do any masonry work when snow, ice or frost covers the footings.

Always cover tops of all unfinished walls when work is not in progress. Never allow the top of a wall to be soaked with rain, snow or frost. If same does occur it should be allowed to dry out before continuing work. Skilled masons seldom allow this to happen and when it does they use live steam to eliminate ice.

ERECT BATTER BOARDS

If you are building a long wall, terrace or laying a walk on a slope, to insure digging trenches and laying a wall straight, level, or at pitch project requires, and at exact distance from house or property line job requires, set up batter boards and guide lines.

First decide what grade level you want around finished project. Drive a stake flush into ground at a point that indicates the finished grade you want. This is called the grade level stake, Illus. 66. Drive a 6 penny nail into top of this stake, allowing nail to project 1″ above. Tie a line to nail and stretch the line over area selected for your project. This will tell you the high and low places. Place a line level on line. Note high and low points. This will give you some idea of where to remove soil, where to fill in.

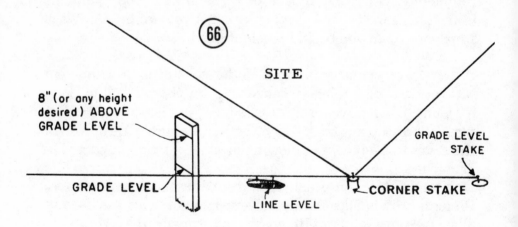

Next drive a stake into ground to indicate a corner. This stake can project 3″ to 4″ above grade. Drive a nail into the top of the stake.

48

Approximately 3′ from this corner stake, drive a batter board stake. Use 1x4's sharpened at one end. Batter board stakes can project above top edge of batter boards or be sawed off flush as shown. Stretch a line from the grade level stake to the batter board stake. Attach level to line. When line reads level, mark stake. This mark now indicates "grade level."

To establish a trenching guide line, hook the end of a steel measuring tape to nail in corner stake and measure exact distance. Drive a stake to indicate exact corner. 3′ from this corner stake erect three batter board stakes, Illus. 67.

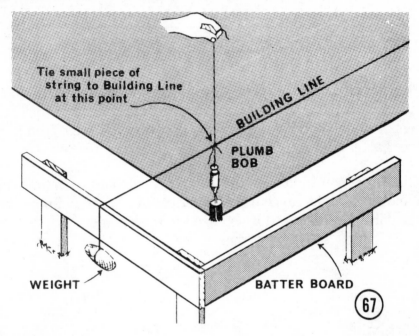

Now check distance this line is from your house or property line to make certain it's parallel to, or at right angle to property line, or distance local codes require. Next nail batter boards to stakes. The top edge of batter board must be level.

If you are laying out a large patio or terrace, a layout square, Illus. 68, helps establish guide lines. This can be 3′x4′x5′, or 6′x8′x 10′. To make a layout square, square off ends of a 1x4. Mark 3′ on one board, 4′ on another, 5′ on a third; or 6′, 8′ and 10′. Nail or screw boards together as shown.

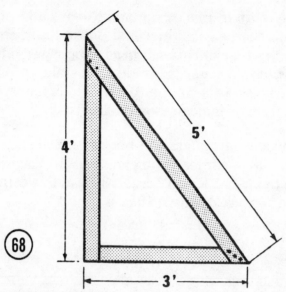

Place layout square parallel to your first guide line. Sight down square. Stretch guide lines above nails that indicate exact corners. A plumb bob helps locate exact corner, Illus. 69. Run lines over batter boards and only tie them temporarily.

These lines now indicate outside edge. Next check each line with a line level. Make saw cuts in batter board to lower a line; drive a nail into batter board if you need to raise a line.

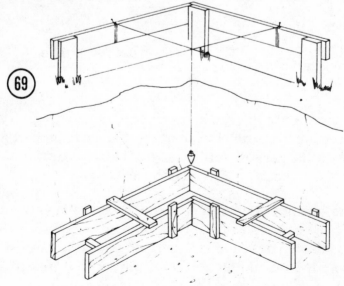

To make certain lines are square, measure diagonals, Illus. 70. Lines are considered square when diagonals measure equal length. When lines are square and level, tie a piece of string to line to indicate exact corners.

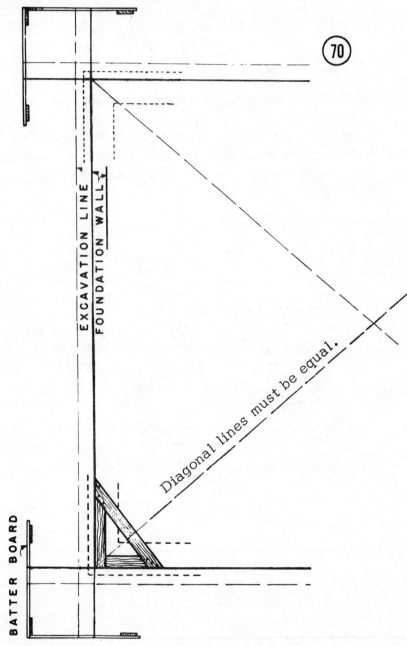

When lines are level and square, they provide a guide that permits digging foundation trenches. If you are digging by hand, the lines won't be in the way. If you dig by machine, lines will have to be moved an exact distance away to allow equipment to work. On large jobs a builder will spread a ribbon of flour directly under line. The lines are temporarily removed to allow equipment to dig. After excavating, the lines are replaced to permit setting footing forms to the line.

If you are building a wall to enclose a garden, or laying a foundation for a terrace, decide whether you will want to run service lines through the footing before laying concrete. Illus. 71 shows a drain tile across a footing. After footings have set up, water, electric, telephone, T.V., heating or outdoor wiring can be run through tile before paving.

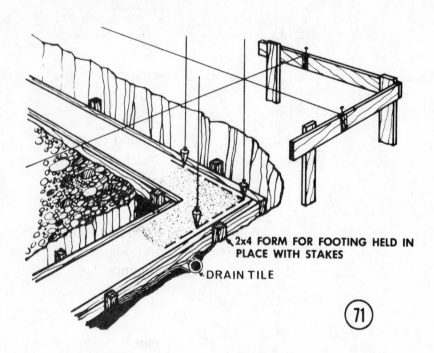

2x4 FORM FOR FOOTING HELD IN PLACE WITH STAKES

DRAIN TILE

71

Since the frost level differs, and in many areas there's none at all, always build footing forms on undisturbed soil, at a depth that meets local code requirements.

If the site is level and firm, and you are building a free-standing brick wall, 2x4's can be used for footing forms, Illus. 71. Always make certain footing forms are level or sloped to pitch required. Mix concrete as outlined on page 10. Use a 2x4 as a screed to level concrete in form, Illus. 72.

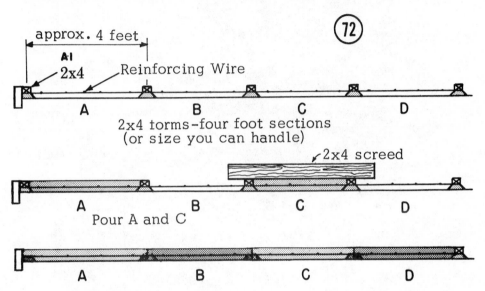

(72)

approx. 4 feet

A1

2x4   Reinforcing Wire

A   B   C   D

2x4 forms—four foot sections
(or size you can handle)

2x4 screed

A   B   C   D
Pour A and C

A   B   C   D

Remove forms and pour sections B and D. Fill in area between A1 and form. Second pouring is indicated by darker shading.

PIER AND PANEL GARDEN WALL

A 4" brick wall, Illus. 8, is one of the most popular ways to fence in your property. It eliminates children and dogs from rampaging in restricted areas; provides a maintenance free, no paint fence, one that usually eliminates property line arguments with nosey new neighbors.

A 4" thick, 8'0" high brick wall, Illus. 8, can be constructed on top of undisturbed soil. Only footings for pilasters need be placed below frost level, Illus. 73. The success of a thin wall is dependent on the use and spacing of reinforcing steel in the wall, Illus. 74, and in the pilasters. Two reinforcing rods, Illus. 73, should be used in each pilaster as specified, Illus. 75.

(73)

Vertical
Reinforcement
Rods in
Pilaster

Horizontal
Reinforcement Rods
in Bed Joints

(74)

TABLE 1—Panel Wall Reinforcing Steel

Wall Span, ft	Vertical Spacing, in.								
	Wind Load, 10 psf			Wind Load, 15 psf			Wind Load, 20 psf		
	A	B	C	A	B	C	A	B	C
8	45	30	19	30	20	12	23	15	9.5
10	29	19	12	19	13	8.0	14	10	6.0
12	20	13	8.5	13	9.0	5.5	10	7.0	4.0
14	15	10	6.5	10	6.5	4.0	7.5	5.0	3.0
16	11	7.5	5.0	7.5	5.0	3.0	6.0	4.0	2.5

Note:

A = 2 - No. 2 bars
B = 2 - 3/16-in. diam wires
C = 2 - 9 gage wires

Reinforcing steel to be placed in mortar joints may be any one of three types, as identified under A, B, C. They are manufactured by many companies under trade names. Determine cost and availability in your area, then select one.

54

TABLE 2—Pier Reinforcing Steel[1]

Wall Span, ft	Wind Load, 10 psf			Wind Load, 15 psf			Wind Load, 20 psf		
	Wall Height, ft			Wall Height, ft			Wall Height, ft		
	4	6	8	4	6	8	4	6	8
8	2#3	2#4	2#5	2#3	2#5	2#6	2#4	2#5	2#5
10	2#3	2#4	2#5	2#4	2#5	2#7	2#4	2#6	2#6
12	2#3	2#5	2#6	2#4	2#6	2#6	2#4	2#6	2#7
14	2#3	2#5	2#6	2#4	2#6	2#6	2#5	2#5	2#7
16	2#4	2#5	2#7	2#4	2#6	2#7	2#5	2#6	2#7

(75)

[1] Within heavy lines 12 by 16-in. pier required. All other values obtained with 12 by 12-in. pier

Use two No. 4 rods in each pilaster for a 6 foot high, 8'0" span; two No. 5 rods in each pilaster when building an 8'0" high wall. These specifications refer to a wind load of 10 pounds per square foot of area (psf). When building an 8'0" high wall with a clear span of 12'0" or 14'0", pilasters should be 12"x16". Use two No. 6 reinforcing rods as shown in Illus. 75.

Note the three different ways you can lock a 4" brick wall to pilasters, Illus. 76. Pilasters can be 12"x12" as shown.

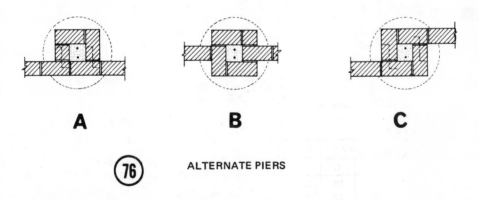

A   **B**   **C**

(76)   ALTERNATE PIERS

The design for the pier and garden wall, Illus. 8, and Tables 1, 2, 3, pages 54, 55, 56 is in compliance with the Recommended Building Code Requirements for Engineered Brick Masonry SCPI, May 1966; and "Building Code Requirements for R - inforced Masonry", USAS A41. 2—1960. The pier found- ation diameter and required embedment below grade are based upon an avarage allowable soil pressure of 3000psf.

The size of piers (footings) for various size pilasters is shown in Illus. 77, 78. For example, an 8'0" span, 4'0" high, requires an 18" diameter footing, at least 2'0" deep. In areas where there's frost, always dig down below frost level.

TABLE 3—Required Embedment for Pier Foundation[1]

Wall Span, ft	Wind Load, 10 psf			Wind Load, 15 psf			Wind Load, 20 psf		
	Wall Height, ft			Wall Height, ft			Wall Height, ft		
	4	6	8	4	6	8	4	6	8
8	2'-0"	2'-3"	2'-9"	2'-3"	2'-6"	3'-0"	2'-3"	2'-9"	3'-0"
10	2'-0"	2'-6"	2'-9"	2'-3"	2'-9"	3'-3"	2'-6"	3'-0"	3'-3"
12	2'-3"	2'-6"	3'-0"	2'-3"	3'-0"	3'-3"	2'-6"	3'-3"	3'-6"
14	2'-3"	2'-9"	3'-0"	2'-6"	3'-0"	3'-3"	2'-9"	3'-3"	3'-9"
16	2'-3"	2'-9"	3'-0"	2'-6"	3'-3"	3'-6"	2'-9"	3'-3"	4'-0"

[1] Within heavy lines 24-in. diam foundation required. All other values obtained with 18-in. diam foundation

(77)

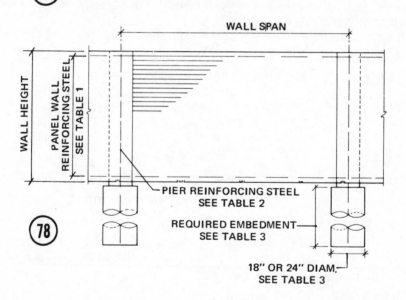

WALL SPAN

WALL HEIGHT

PANEL WALL REINFORCING STEEL SEE TABLE 1

PIER REINFORCING STEEL SEE TABLE 2

REQUIRED EMBEDMENT— SEE TABLE 3

18" OR 24" DIAM. SEE TABLE 3

(78)

When erecting a 14', or larger span, 8' high, 24" diameter footings should go down a minimum of 36", or below frost level. Dig holes for piers at every corner, or turn of the fence, and at every intermediate location span requires. A post hole digger simplifies digging. If the wall is to butt against a house, no pier is required adjacent to house, but end of wall must be anchored to house.

The diameter and depth of each pier, and it's location, is dependent on the wind load, wall height, wall span, depth of frost level. You can build this wall over recently filled or graded soil if you dig holes for piers down to undisturbed soil and to depth recommended.

After digging holes in position, size, and to depth pilasters require, scrape area between pilasters level. While the mortar bed for the first course of brick can be laid on undisturbed soil, we recommend laying first course on an oiled 2x4 placed just below grade. Use length required to butt against pilaster. After wall has been allowed to set a week, the 2x4 can be removed.

As Illus. 76A indicates the wall can be erected flush with pilaster. Since the pilaster must be placed inside your property line, it can be erected as shown in Illus. 76A, B or C, Illus. 79.

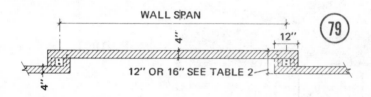

After digging holes to depth required, drive two steel rods in position, Illus. 73. These should be driven into ground. Use length required to extend to top of pilaster. Fill pier holes with concrete containing 1 part Portland cement, 3 parts sand to 5 parts crushed stone. Use a soft mixture to make certain concrete locks to reinforcing rods.

Use Type S mortar made from 1 part Portland cement, ½ part hydrated lime, 3½ to 4½ parts of sand. Lay and lock bricks for pilaster in position shown, Illus. 76, as you lay up each course.

Two #2 reinforcing wires are laid on the top of the first course of brick, and on courses at height indicated in Illus. 74.

Illus. 80 shows actual size of reinforcing rods specified.

REINFORCING WIRE

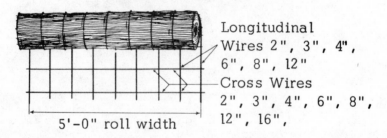

Longitudinal
Wires 2", 3", 4",
6", 8", 12"
Cross Wires
2", 3", 4", 6", 8",
12", 16",

5'-0" roll width

ELECTRICALLY WELDED WIRE FABRIC REINFORCING

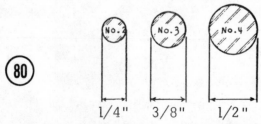

No.2 No.3 No.4

(80)

1/4" 3/8" 1/2"

If you are building an 8' span, where wind loads don't exceed 10 pounds per sq. ft., use 2 #2 bars on courses 45" apart; or two ³⁄₁₆ diameter wire 30" apart; or two #9 gage wire on every 7th course. Position the reinforcing approximately 1" in from end and edge of brick.

As the wall rises, the pilaster is grouted with same mortar used to lay brick. Add sufficient water to allow grout to flow freely around vertical steel. When a wall is built adjacent to a house, use metal ties to secure wall to house. These should be placed in bed joints every 2'0".

Your mason supply retailer can recommend and supply the kind of reinforcing required. If local codes require reinforcing other than that specified, show them the industry recommended specifications, Illus. 74, 75, 77, and let them tell you what to use.

RETAINING WALLS

If you are building a retaining wall, Illus. 81, dig trenches for footings to depth required to go below frost level.

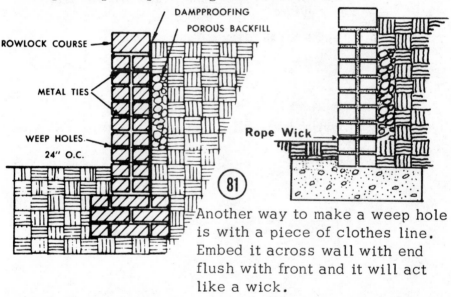

ROWLOCK COURSE

DAMPPROOFING

POROUS BACKFILL

METAL TIES

WEEP HOLES
24" O.C.

Rope Wick

(81)

Another way to make a weep hole is with a piece of clothes line. Embed it across wall with end flush with front and it will act like a wick.

Check bottom of trench with a level and straight edge, Illus. 82. Figure 10½" for each 4 courses, if ⅜" mortar joints are used; 4 courses to 11", if ½" bed joints are used. You can lay bricks for a footing or pour concrete, Illus. 83. We recommend concrete.

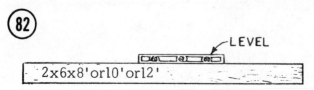

(82)

LEVEL

2x6x8'or10'or12'

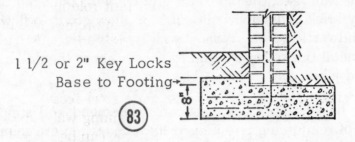

1 1/2 or 2" Key Locks
Base to Footing

(83)

If you are building on a sloping grade, or on rock, use ⅝ or ¾ plyscord to build forms, Illus. 84. Sharpen 2x4 stakes to a point and use these where ground permits driving. Use 1x2 as spreaders. When building a form on rock, saw plyscord to shape rock requires. Use 2x4 as stiffeners. Use 1x2 A as spreaders at top and bottom. Drill holes through plyscord and only drive nails a short way into 1x2 spreader. This permits pulling nails and removing spreaders after you start pouring concrete.

Drill holes through C and run wire around both stakes in position shown. Remove bottom spreader as soon as the concrete begins to fill bottom of form. Allow concrete to set three days, cut wires and remove forms. When you strip the forms, cut wire again, close to footing.

Use 2 x 4B as stiffeners
on top of rock, or as stakes
where ground permits.

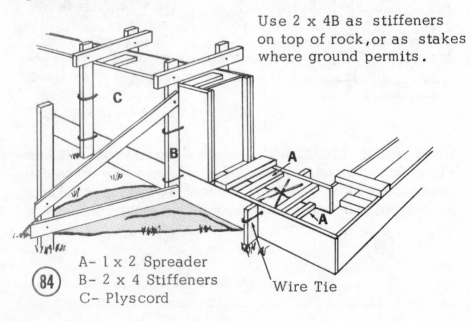

(84)   A- 1 x 2 Spreader
       B- 2 x 4 Stiffeners
       C- Plyscord

Wire Tie

The size of a footing plays an important role in the construction of a retaining wall. The use of reinforcing steel provides great strength with less bulk.

For walls up to 6 feet in height, note steel recommended for RBM — reinforced brick masonry retaining walls in Illus. 85. Because a retaining wall, even a low one, can be subjected to a wide variety of loading conditions, two types of walls are listed.

M represents a medium load; H is for heavy-duty walls.

Medium-duty construction can be used where there is no heavy load, like a driveway, closer to the wall than 1½ times its height.

Use heavy duty reinforcing steel when you plan to build foundations for a building, or driveway, within a distance less than 1½ times the height of the wall.

Illus. 85, 86, specify size of footings recommended and placement of wall on footing. Note distance X, Illus. 86, it's important. Because of the eccentricity of excessive forces, the wall is placed closer to the bank on heavy duty walls. A 3′ high wall is moved in on footing, 2″ closer to the bank.

A retaining wall requires a lot of steel reinforcing positioned where it will do the most good. It must be embedded in mortar consisting of 1 part Portland cement, ¼ part lime and between 2¼ to 3 parts sand. The grout, Illus. 45, used to fill between tiers, may be the same as mortar used to lay brick with this exception. Add pea gravel equal in volume to twice the amount of Portland cement. The pea gravel should be graded with not more than 5% passing through a #8 (³⁄₁₆) sieve, and 95% passing through a ⅜″ sieve.

STEEL REQUIRED FOR LOW RBM RETAINING WALLS.

WALL HEIGHT (H)	BASE WIDTH (W)	LOADING	MIN. DISTANCE (x)	VERTICAL BARS (a)	HORIZONTAL BARS (b)	BASE REINFORCING (c)	BASE REINFORCING (d)
3 Feet	1'-9"	M	4"	#3 @ 24"	2—#4	2—#2	#3 @ 20"
		H	6"	#3 @ 15"	2—#4	2—#2	#3 @ 20"
4 Feet	2'-5"	M	7"	#3 @ 24"	3—#4	2—#2	#3 @ 20"
		H	9"	#4 @ 18"	3—#4	2—#2	#3 @ 20"
5 Feet	3'-0"	M	10"	#3 @ 15"	3—#4	2—#3	#3 @ 15"
		H	12"	#4 @ 12"*	3—#4	2—#3	#3 @ 15"
6 Feet	3'-7"	M	13"	#4 @ 15"	4—#4	2—#3	#4 @ 15"
		H	16"	#4 @ 8'*	4—#4	2—#3	#4 @ 15"

* Alternate bars may be cut off at one-half wall height.

85

62

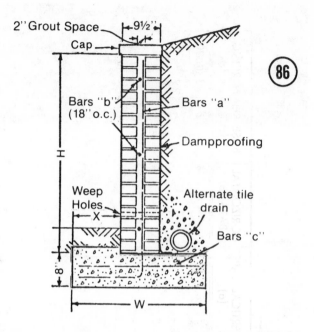

2" Grout Space

9½"

Cap

Bars "b" (18" o.c.)

Bars "a"

Dampproofing

H

Weep Holes

X

Alternate tile drain

Bars "c"

8"

W

(86)

To grout between tiers, it's necessary to add sufficient water to allow grout to fill all joints, crevices, and to completely bond around reinforcing steel, etc., but don't spill grout on face of brick.

A reinforced wall requires careful workmanship to make certain both the front and rear tier of bricks (wythes) are laid with full head and bed joints, and that both wythes are reinforced with cavity wall ties, Illus. 24, 87, 88, plus rods placed vertically in grouted area, Illus. 23.

(87)

Rectangular Tie

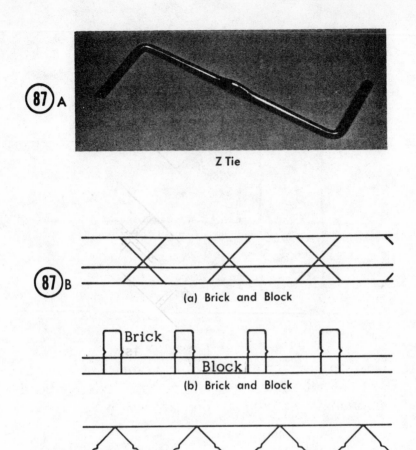

Z Tie

(a) Brick and Block

Brick

Block

(b) Brick and Block

(c) Brick and Brick

To start, embed reinforcing rods, size determined by specification shown in Illus. 85, in footings in position shown, Illus. 83. Bend rod vertically as shown.

Lay first three courses on one tier, 4 courses on other tier, then pour and puddle grout around rods. Stop pouring grout about a 1½″ below lower course. Use a 1x2 planed to a dull knife edge to puddle grout. This eliminates air pockets and voids.

Space reinforcing bars "b", Illus. 86, every 18″ on centers. Space vertical bars "a" every 24″, or spacing indicated, Illus. 85.

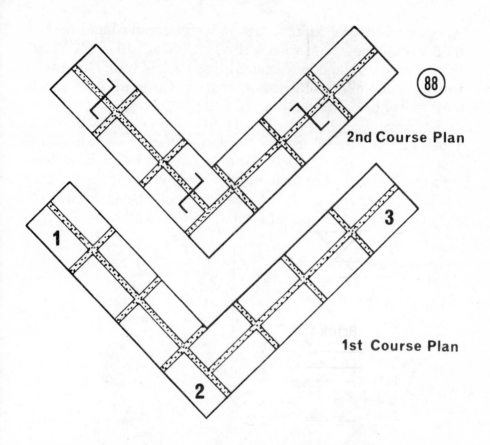

2nd Course Plan

1st Course Plan

1   2   3

To permit wall to drain properly, weep holes the size of half a brick should be positioned in bottom course every four to six feet. One way to make weep holes is to cut a 2x4x4". Oil it thoroughly. Drive an 8 penny nail in the front edge, Illus. 89. Allow nail to project ½". Place these in position as you would a half brick. When grout has been allowed to set thoroughly (one week), use pliers and carefully pull 2x4 out. If you want to make an exact size opening, nail a piece of ¾ to 2x4. ¾" plus 1½" (thickness of 2x4) should equal thickness of brick.

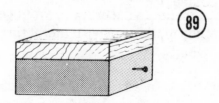

Another method of making certain water doesn't build up behind a retaining wall is with a "French Drain," Illus. 86. Place these end to end, about ½″ apart, along back of wall. Run these to a dry well. Cover joints with roofing felt. Cover tile with about 6″ of gravel before backfilling, Illus. 90.

When building a wall in an area that's recently been filled or graded, always dig footings down to undisturbed soil. If this isn't possible, lay #2 or #3 reinforcing rods in footings. Use 2x8 or 2x10 for forms. Lay 3½″ of concrete, then place two rows of rods. Overlap ends of rods at least 4″ to 6″, Illus. 90.

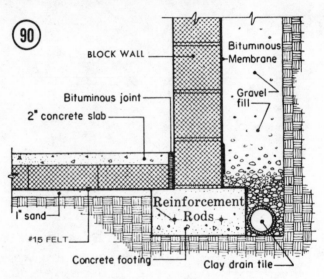

BRICK VENEER OVER EXISTING CLAPBOARD OR SHINGLE

Brick veneering is easy to apply if you allow a minimum 1″ space between existing siding, Illus. 91. Many pros nail a 1x2 or ¾ x 2″ brick mold across header and casings of a window, then butt veneer against mold, Illus. 92. The brick mold is usually of sufficent thickness to project veneer away from corner boards. Anchor veneer to studs in framing with metal ties, Illus. 10, 91, using 8 penny common nails.

When applying brick to an existing structure, you must first excavate to depth of footings. Build new foundation wall using

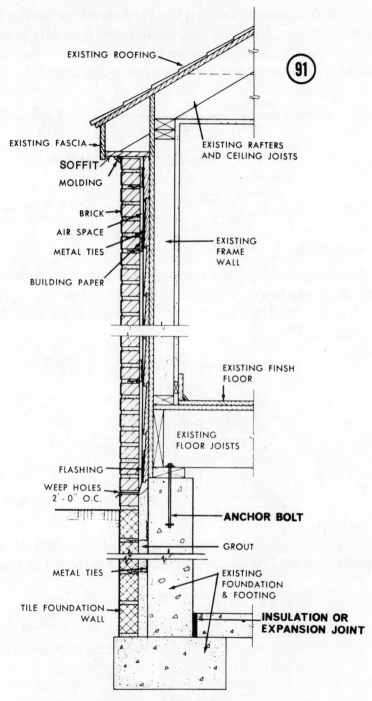

EXISTING ROOFING

91

EXISTING FASCIA

SOFFIT

MOLDING

BRICK

AIR SPACE

METAL TIES

BUILDING PAPER

EXISTING RAFTERS
AND CEILING JOISTS

EXISTING
FRAME
WALL

EXISTING FINSH
FLOOR

EXISTING
FLOOR JOISTS

FLASHING

WEEP HOLES
2'-0" O.C.

ANCHOR BOLT

GROUT

METAL TIES

EXISTING
FOUNDATION
& FOOTING

TILE FOUNDATION
WALL

**INSULATION OR
EXPANSION JOINT**

TYPICAL WALL SECTION
NEW MASONRY VENEER OVER EXISTING WALL

4″x8″x16″ concrete blocks up to grade level, or build a form and pour concrete. In either case anchor new foundation to existing one with 1″ wide, 22 gauge metal ties, every 16″ vertically, and every 25″ horizontally. Use steel cut nails, Illus. 93.

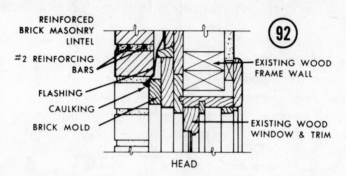

HEAD

If existing footings don't provide a shoulder as shown in Illus. 91, dig down to a depth equal to bottom of existing footings, and set up a form. Pour a new footing 6″ wide along each wall to be veneered, Illus. 93.

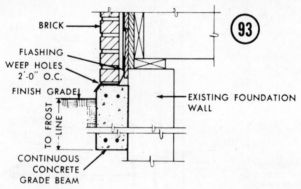

If conditions prevent excavating down to footings, an alternate method of anchoring the starter course is shown in Illus. 94.

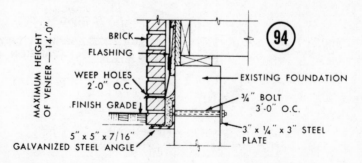

In this application a 5″x5″x⁷⁄₁₆″ galvanized steel angle is bolted the entire length of foundation with ¾″x10″ bolts every 3′0″. A ¼″x3″x3″ steel plate on inside provides needed bearing under nut. Use a ¾″ or ⅞″ carbide tipped masonry drill. Drill holes below grade level. The angle must be fastened full length of wall.

An easier way is to drill ½″ or ¾″ holes every three feet through mortar joints in wall, then inserting a ½″ or ¾″ x 12″ reinforcing rod through each hole. Allow rod to project distance required to support angle iron. Wire angle iron to rods. Lay first course of brick in mortar. This will bury wires holding rods. Use a truss tie or ladder tie, or equal reinforcing in bed over first course, Illus. 95.

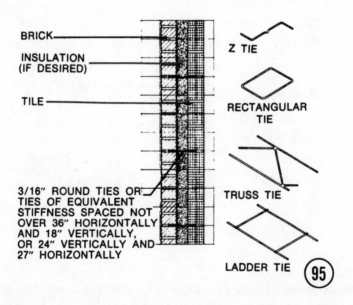

BRICK

INSULATION (IF DESIRED)

TILE

3/16″ ROUND TIES OR TIES OF EQUIVALENT STIFFNESS SPACED NOT OVER 36″ HORIZONTALLY AND 18″ VERTICALLY, OR 24″ VERTICALLY AND 27″ HORIZONTALLY

Z TIE

RECTANGULAR TIE

TRUSS TIE

LADDER TIE 95

Use a gage stick or story pole to ascertain width of mortar joints and number of courses needed to fit under windows, Illus. 96. Note brick sill. This can be made with cut bricks under a wood window sill, Illus. 96, or under a steel or aluminum frame, Illus. 97. Always install flashing where noted.

Bricks laid under a window can be cut for a rowlock, Illus. 1, or a header course. Note pitch indicated, Illus. 96.

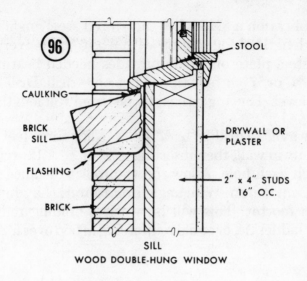

STOOL

CAULKING

BRICK
SILL

DRYWALL OR
PLASTER

FLASHING

2" x 4" STUDS
16" O.C.

BRICK

SILL
WOOD DOUBLE-HUNG WINDOW

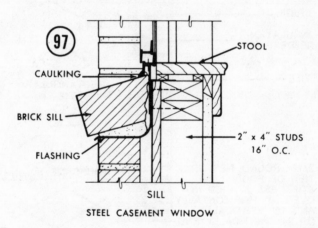

STOOL

CAULKING

BRICK SILL

2" x 4" STUDS
16" O.C.

FLASHING

SILL
STEEL CASEMENT WINDOW

Copper flashing, Illus. 91, should be installed on top of first course above grade; or on top of footing, Illus. 93. Nail flashing to framing with copper nails.

Using a mortar mix containing 1 part Portland cement, ½ part lime, to 4½ parts of sand, lay mortar bed at, or below, grade level.

Copper flashing is recommended since it's most compatible to mortar. Flashing must extend through brick facing as shown, under windows, Illus. 96.

Brick veneer should be anchored to studs with metal ties Illus. 98, 9, 10 and 11.

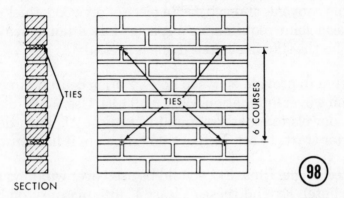

SECTION

TIES

TIES

6 COURSES

98

Corner poles are the key to applying brick veneer. If you plan on facing two or more walls, set up corner poles, Illus. 99. As previously recommended, always get corner pole manufacturer's directions when you buy or rent corner poles. They provide many valuable time saving tips. Use a plumb bob and framing square to locate exact position of a corner pole, Illus. 99.

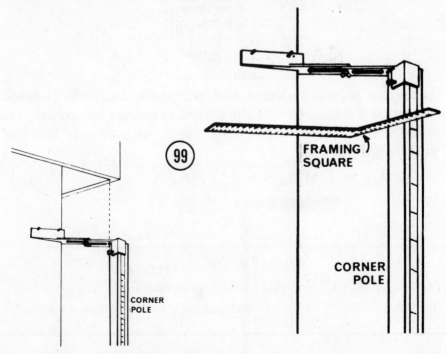

FRAMING SQUARE

99

CORNER POLE

CORNER POLE

Always take time to lay bricks out dry to check exact size head joint you need for the first course. Tighten up or expand head joints to avoid cutting brick. Before mixing mortar, place bricks within convenient reach. Use a piece of plywood, thickness equal to head joint required, as a spacer. Lay a fairly heavy mortar bed for the starting course if one is needed.

Be sure to provide ⅜″ weep holes, 2′0″ on center, directly above flashing over foundation, Illus. 91, 93, 94. Use ⅜″x6″ oiled dowels. Cut dowels to length required to project 2″. Turn dowel after mortar starts to set. Remove dowel before it hardens.

A steel angle, Illus. 100, should be used over windows and doors as a lintel. Extend these at least 4″ into masonry on both sides of opening. Note position of flashing.

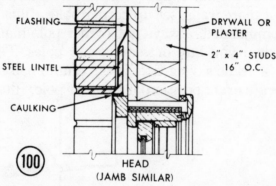

FLASHING — DRYWALL OR PLASTER

2″ x 4″ STUDS 16″ O.C.

STEEL LINTEL

CAULKING

(100)   HEAD
(JAMB SIMILAR)

There are several different and acceptable methods of brick veneering a house. One of the easiest is to remove molding on gable fascia, Illus. 101, leaving fascia in position. Remove gutters and leaders.

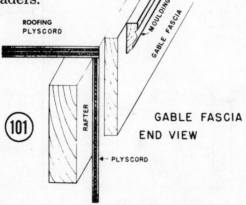

ROOFING PLYSCORD

MOULDING

GABLE FASCIA

RAFTER

(101)   GABLE FASCIA
END VIEW

PLYSCORD

If you want to project bricks over edge of casing to gain space needed for a Rowlock sill course, it's OK. Use metal brick ties on every other course to secure bricks adjacent to a window.

When brick veneering a house with a porch, canopy or patio, use a 5"x5"x$\frac{7}{16}$" angle to support the first course of brick over the roof. Drill $\frac{3}{8}$" holes through angle, in position required to fasten it every 16" to studs in wall. Use $\frac{3}{8}$x1$\frac{1}{2}$" lag screws. Drill $\frac{1}{4}$" holes in studs to receive lag screws. Fasten angle following pitch of roof. Cut end bricks to angle required.

Proper caulking around all window and door frames is essential to the success of a brick veneer application. Use a caulking gun, Illus. 102.

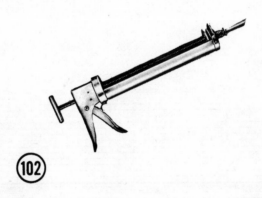

(102)

After laying brick adjacent to a window or door casing, and while mortar is still plastic, notch the mortar joint by shoving a piece of $\frac{1}{4}$" plywood $\frac{3}{4}$" into joint. Do this the full length of the casing. Fill this continuous $\frac{1}{4}$"x$\frac{3}{4}$" slot with silicone or other elastic caulking compound. Use a pressure gun to make certain joint is completely filled.

Be sure to protect a partially completed wall against moisture. Cover walls every night with plastic to keep them dry. Allow covering polyethylene to drop down at least two feet.

When you brick veneer the front of many houses, the brick butts against the soffit, Illus. 91. Since you actually extend the length of the house when brick is added to gable ends, the roof must be extended over gable ends to cover veneer. In new construction the roof sheathing goes on after framing is completed. The sheathing on roof overhangs gable ends 5″, 6″ or 7″ or exact amount needed, Illus. 103, to cover brick veneer.

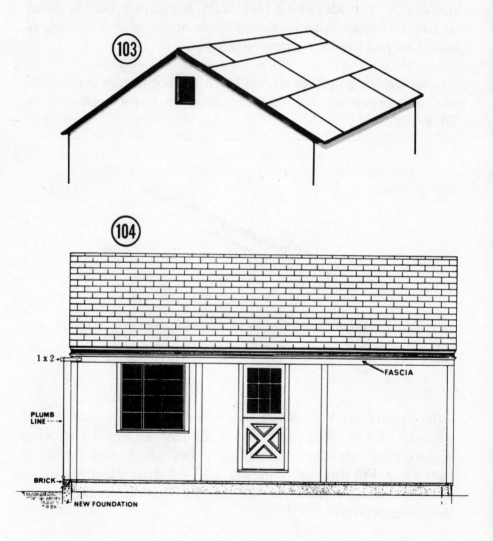

To ascertain exact amount of overhang, a brick is placed on foundation in position veneer requires, Illus. 104. To estimate exact roof overhang, nail a 1x2 to fascia across front. Drop a plumb bob down from 1x2. When point of bob just barely touches outside edge of brick, the 1x2 is marked. The roof sheathing on new construction is sawed along this line. When veneering is completed, the fascia board, nailed to edge of sheathing, extends 1½" below top edge of veneer. When you apply brick veneer over existing clapboard or shingle, you must also extend the roof sheathing, roofing shingles, and apply a new fascia.

First apply #15 roofing felt over side to be veneered. Overlap courses 2". Remove trim if there is any on fascia.

Estimate exact distance brick veneer will project beyond siding. If, for example, the plumb bob indicates 5", cut 2x4 blocks 4", or 4¼"; length depends on thickness of lumber you use. Make up a sample. Cut a 2x4x4". Nail a scrap piece of 1x4A to 2x4 block, Illus. 105.

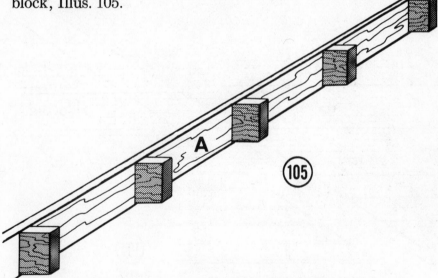

Nail a piece of plyscord roof sheathing B, Illus. 106.

Nail a piece of 1x6 (fascia) C, in position, to edge of B, Illus. 107.

Place assembled sample against existing fascia. Drop a plumb bob down. Point of bob should just miss edge of brick, Illus. 104. Readjust length of 2x4 if necessary.

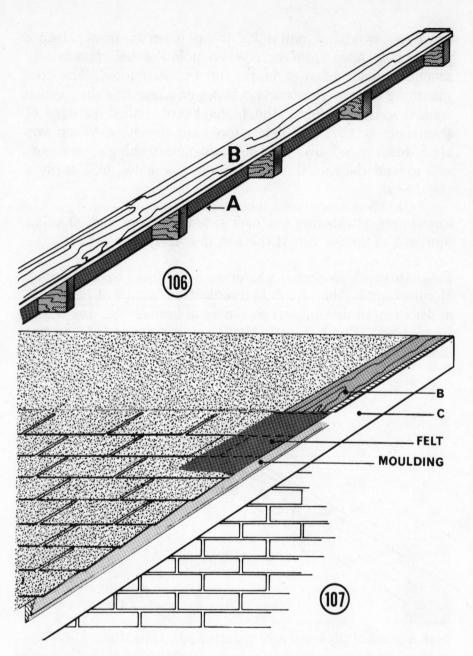

When you have established the proper length of 2x4 blocking, cut as many as you need. These are nailed in position to 1x4 every 16″. The first one, Illus. 105, is nailed in position flush and plumb with front fascia. All others are positioned flush with top edge of A. Use 1x4x12′ or lengths needed to cover existing fascia on gable ends. Nail through A into 2x4 blocking with two 8 penny common nails.

Next cut ½, ⅝ or ¾ plyscord sheathing (use thickness equal to that on roof), to width of assembled 1x4 and 2x4, by length required, Illus. 106. Nail B in position. Keeping B flush with sheathing on roof, nail through A into existing fascia with 8 or 10 penny nails.

Apply veneer, Illus. 108. When veneering is completed, and allowed to set at least a week, paint both sides of fascia board C with exterior paint. When dry, nail new fascia to edge of B, Illus. 107. Use width required to allow fascia to overlap veneer 1½". Counter sink nail heads. Fill holes with putty or wood filler. Paint with exterior paint.

Loosen up and remove nails holding edge shingles. Cut strips of No. 15 roofing felt to width required to slip under felt on roof and to finish flush with outside edge of new fascia. Staple felt to sheathing.

Nail new and old roofing shingles in position. Allow shingles to project over edge of new fascia 1", or a distance equal to projection on old roof. Use asphalt roofing cement to fill any holes you made when you loosened up existing shingles.

WALKS, PATIO, EDGING

A brick walk, patio or edging around a garden, Illus. 109, 110, 111, can be laid dry in sand, in the same manner they were done during Colonial times, with one exception. When laying a walk or patio, #15 roofing felt, Illus. 112, is now laid over 1" or 2" of tamped sand. This acts as a weed deterent. After all bricks are laid in pattern selected, dry sand is swept into joints. As it filters down, more is added each week until joints are completely sealed.

If water collects, you can do two things. Punch small holes in felt and water will drain off in sand. A preventative method is to lay a clothes line on top of sand before applying felt. Line acts like a wick. Low end will drip water.

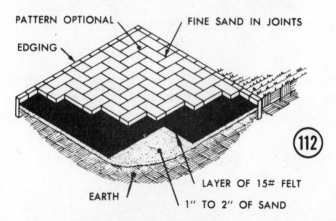

PATTERN OPTIONAL   FINE SAND IN JOINTS

EDGING

EARTH

LAYER OF 15# FELT

1" TO 2" OF SAND

The edge of a paved area can be laid up before or after paving is completed. It can be laid against undisturbed soil or in concrete, Illus. 113. Paint 1x6 or 2x8 forms with old crankcase oil and set to angle walk requires. Leave form in place after setting the edging, and use it with a straight edge to check paving to height and pitch it requires. While edging around a flower bed can be set and held in place with well tamped soil, edging for most walks, patios, tree wells, etc., should be set in concrete, even when the paving area is laid over sand.

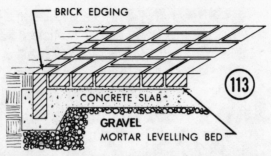

BRICK EDGING

CONCRETE SLAB

GRAVEL

MORTAR LEVELLING BED

FLOOR PAVING OVER CONCRETE SLAB

The first step, after staking out the site, is to set up guide lines to identify exact area to be paved. Next decide what slope (pitch) is required to provide drainage without creating new problems. Also consider whether area to be paved will finish flush with existing grade or be raised above. To simplify cutting grass, many walks and terraces are finished flush, or at a height that permits running mower over edging, Illus. 114.

Excavate area to a depth that permits spreading 1″ to 1½″ of gravel or crushed stone, 1″ to 1½″ of concrete, plus ½″ to 1″ of mortar. Excavate trench for edging to approximately 6″ to 10″. Set up 1x6, 2x6, or 2x8 forms to pitch job requires. Set a sailor course, or style edging desired, in concrete. Keep edging flush with top of form.

80

Walks and terraces adjacent to a house must slope away from house. A pitch of ⅛" to a foot is usually sufficient. The outside edge of a 3 foot wide walk would be ⅜" lower than edge adjacent to house. The outside edge would be ¾" lower if pitched ¼" per foot. Always consider whether the paved area will act as a catch basin or causeway, and provide pitch and drainage needed.

Use a flat shovel or edger, to set brick edging in a soil base. Excavate entire area to depth paving requires. If brick is laid over well tamped sand, only thickness of brick and 1" to 2" of sand represents depth of paved area. Never dig deeper than required. When brick is set in sand placed over undisturbed soil, it has a good chance of staying in place. Tamp sand over a back filled base and settling can cause trouble. It's never wise to lay brick paving over any recently back filled area. If site is questionable, a 3" reinforced concrete slab, poured over well tamped gravel, is recommended. Never use a sand bed. But even a reinforced slab will settle if soil below continues to compact.

When paving an area where underground moisture might prove troublesome, spread polyethylene, Illus. 115, over ground. Use 6x6 reinforcing wire. Raise wire 1" above polyethylene using globs of concrete every 4 feet.

GRAVEL ⌐ WATERPROOF MEMBRANE ⌐ 6"X6"WIRE ⌐

The easiest way to slope paving to pitch drainage requires, is to set up forms so top edge is placed at pitch required, Illus. 72. Use globs of concrete to set forms to height required. You can do this in two stages, i.e. set up 2x4, flat — 1½" for a 1½" concrete slab. Pitch 2x4 to angle and height slab requires. Using a 2x4 screed, Illus. 72, level concrete to pitch of form. After concrete begins to set, frequently within an hour, score slab with a stick, Illus. 116.

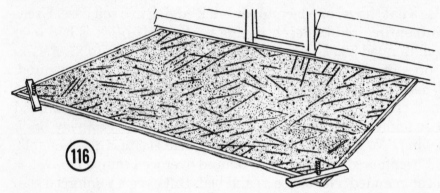

(116)

Allow concrete to set two to three days, then toenail 2x4's edgewise, to top of forms. Since 2x4 usually measures 3½", use it full width or cut to width needed so top edge represents finished face of brick paving. By placing a straight edge across form, you can lay brick paving to exact pitch needed. If edging is to finish flush with paving, place it in position. Lay edging last, after removing forms, if edging is to be raised higher than paving.

Always paint forms with old crankcase oil before using to keep concrete from sticking. Never drive nails all the way in when making forms. Always allow grouted paving to set a week before removing forms.

ADDITIONAL FACTS

When laying a large slab, it's usually necessary to set forms every 3 to 4 feet apart. This permits screeding concrete in smaller sections. Illus. 72, shows forms set up at pitch job requires. Use globs of concrete. If job requires reinforcing wire, it should be raised about 1". As previously mentioned, paint forms with old crankcase oil before setting in position.

Pour section A. Using a 2x4 as a screed, work it back and forth to level concrete to form. After filling, allow this section to set ½ to 1 hour, then remove form A 1. Fill void with concrete. Score section as outlined previously. Next fill section C. Allow section A and C to set sufficiently to support screed before pouring section B and D.

In some paving patterns, 2x4's either flat or on edge, remain permanently in position. Always use pressure-treated lumber or paint 2x4 with wood preservative before placing in position.

One way to do a large area, is to measure the overall area, then divide it into equal size sections, Illus. 118. This shows a section that measures 5 brick square, not counting the border. This section can be repeated any number of times; or any number of bricks could be added or subtracted. You could use fewer or more bricks per course. Or you could start at the exact center of area to be paved with bricks A A, and work out. If you want to start in one corner, and the brick edging is to finish flush with paving, it can be laid first. Set up guide lines and lay edging to line. If brick edging is to act as a curb, do it after paving is completed.

Always begin by leveling and tamping a sand bed to height paving requires, or lay a concrete slab. If you set your forms to pitch paving requires, and to height equal to finished face of paving, Illus. 118, you can make a screed by nailing a 1x4 to a 2x4, Illus. 117. This screed can be made to spread and level sand to height required. Or, as previously mentioned, a two part form can be used to lay a sand bed or a concrete slab.

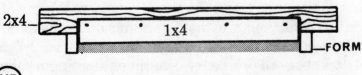

(117) Use 1 x 4 to screed sand.
Use 2 x 4 edge to screed concrete.

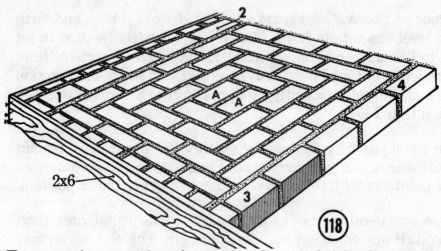

To ascertain exact size of a section, lay out bricks dry. When you get ready to lay a section, position bricks 1 and 2 level with form. After paving is completed, use dry grout to fill all joints.

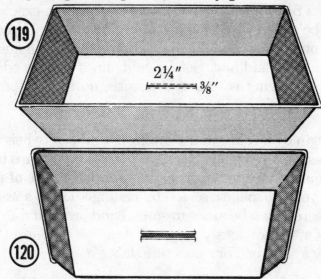

To grout joints, mix 1 part Portland cement to 2 parts of very fine sand. To fill joints without messing up surface, use dry grout. To pour grout easily, cut two ⅜″ wide slots, 2¼″ apart, Illus. 119, in bottom of a coffee can, tin or aluminum cake pan. Bend lips down along dash line, Illus. 120. Pour dry grout into this slotted container and fill joints without messing up surface. Use a piece of ¼″ plywood to pack grout into ⅜″ joints. Use a ⅜″ piece of plywood to pack grout into ½″ joints. When all joints are filled, spray entire surface with a fine mist. Use care not to discharge grout from cracks. Do this every day for three days. Always spray with the finest mist possible. Always point hose up, not on paving. If you find it necessary to add more grout, do so only when paving is bone dry. Repeat procedure outlined.

Allow grouted paving to set a week before removing forms. Use care not to crack any joints, or loosen any brick. If no edging was laid, do it now. Edging can be laid to height desired. Bricks used for edging are frequently set tight, no joints. Again, lay out brick dry to ascertain how it will finish.

Illus. 121 shows a basket weave paving pattern. This can be laid on a sand bed, or in mortar over a concrete slab. Start with edging if same is to finish flush with paving. Position bricks No. 1 and No. 2, then lay course between. Lay brick No. 3 and No. 4 and then the bricks between. When paving is completed, use a straight 2x4 and a hammer to level off any bricks that require same. Fill all joints with sand or with dry grout as previously explained.

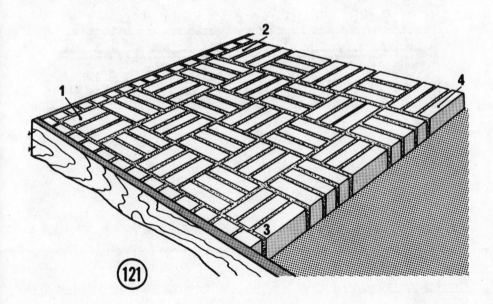

Illus. 122 shows a herringbone paving pattern. You can start this pattern with a brick edging, or do it after paving is completed. After establishing grade levels, and laying a sand or mortar bed, as previously outlined, cut triangular pieces A, Illus. 122. Use the full size pattern, Illus. 123. Cut B, Illus. 124; C, Illus. 125; D, Illus. 126.

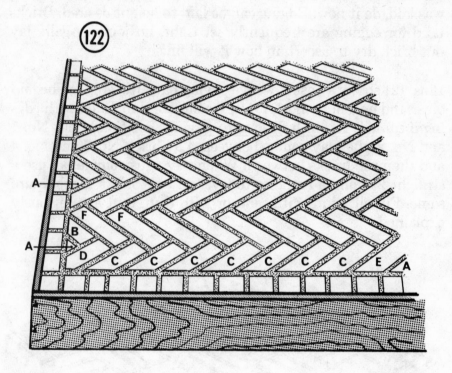

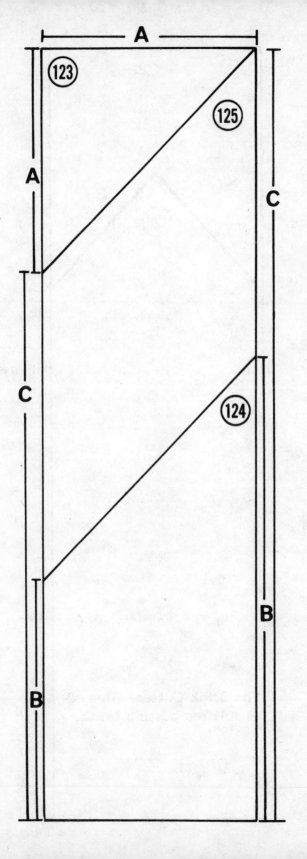

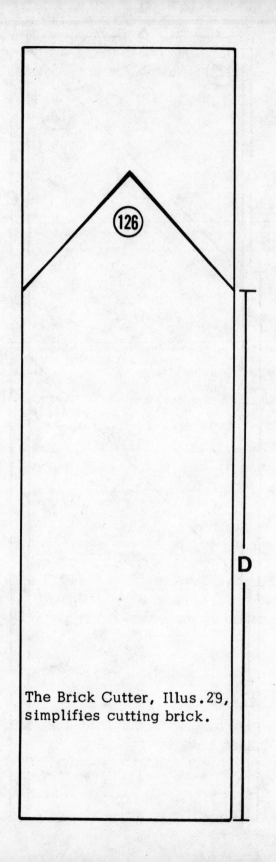

The Brick Cutter, Illus. 29, simplifies cutting brick.

In this job you need a straight edge and a large plastic or wood triangle, Illus. 127.

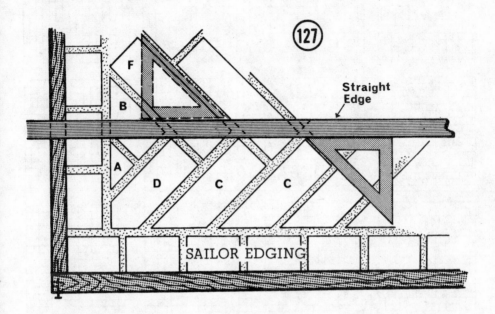

Masonry supply retailers having masonry saws will cut bricks A, B, C and D to shape and length indicated. Or you can do it yourself if you place brick on a sandbag and give the chisel a smart blow.

Start at corner with D, Illus. 127. Space A and B so it lines up with the end of D and F, Illus. 122. F is a full brick that fits into position shown. Always use the straight edge and triangle to line up corners of brick as shown. After laying and grouting all brick, remove forms and set brick edging in concrete if you didn't start job with edging.

Illus. 128 shows other paving patterns that can be laid following the same procedure.

Any of these patterns can be laid with 4″x8″ actual dimension units laid dry and tight, or with mortar joints. Patterns that require the width of the unit to be half the length, must be laid dry and tight.

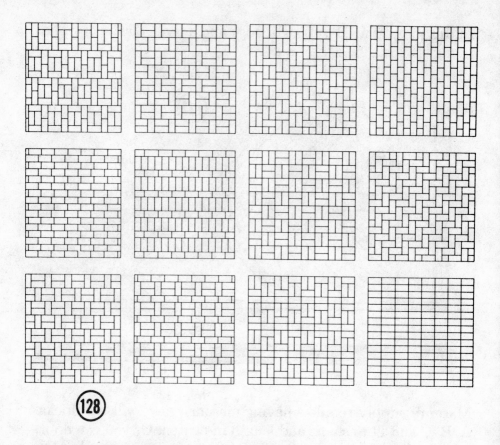

(128)

MORTARLESS BRICK FLOORS

In recent years the "mortarless" brick floor, Illus. 129, has become extremely popular in both remodeling and in new construction. It is easy, fast and cheaper to install than floors laid in mortar. The base may be a concrete slab, or well tamped sand, or over a well sanded level wood floor. Only lay brick on a solid wood floor. Always cover a wood floor with #15 felt after sanding. Staple felt to floor. Do not overlap felt. If a sand bed is laid, use a 2x4 and hammer to level up any high spots after laying brick. Interior brick paving can be sealed with sealants available from your masonry supply retailer. If silicones are used as a sealer, use a 5% solution of solvent-based silicones.

Solvent-based silicones penetrate and dry faster than water-based silicones. After sealing, wax may be applied. Use wax recommended for brick floors. Do not use varnish or shellac.

If you want to produce a designed-styled interior brick floor, finish surface using a terrazzo grinder. These can be rented. Use grade of sandpaper retailer recommends. If you want to polish brick paving, use hard-burred dense brick. You pay a little more, but the results are pure magic. After grinding, apply sealant and wax your brick retailer recommends. Follow manufacturers directions. Invite your neighbors in to see your handiwork and it will put you into business.

Noted decorators invariably use brick extensively when remodeling "town houses." Floors and walls create a rare charm when covered with brick, Illus. 130. Many retailers stock a thin brick for interior floors. These are about 1″ thick. It's necessary to remove door sills, cut door down to height required. Replace sill and rehang door. A brick floor in an entrance hall creates an instant conversation piece.

CLEANING BRICK

Those who prefer grouting, should use extreme care to protect the surface. Most mortar droppings can be removed by immediately wiping with a piece of burlap. If you are real fussy, coat the face of each brick with a silicone sealant before laying. While this is a time consuming and costly way to lay brick, it does help keep them clean. Try not to allow any mortar to harden on the surface. Wipe it away as fast as you can. To remove Portland cement stains, the cleaning solution must be capable of dissolving hardened cement. Many bricklayers use a solution containing muriatic acid. Since acid is harmful to human skin, use great caution. Wear rubber gloves. Protect your eyes and face. Use a long-sleeved shirt and never allow it to come in contact with your clothing. Don't use acid in a closed, heated room. The fumes are harmful to lungs, even corrode metal objects. While muriatic acid will dissolve hardened mortar, it will also eat up grout, so if you use it, use great caution. There are a number of proprietary masonry cleaners available that are far less dangerous. These should be used exactly as the manufacturer recommends. Never use a cleaner full strength. Always dilute it the exact amount the manufacturer specifies. Most cleaners specify spraying the paving with a fine mist until water runs freely over the surface. Wetting fills pores, reduces suction. This simple precaution helps prevent discoloration, stain or "acid burn." Apply cleaner with a small stiff fiber brush. Scrub only a small area at a time, and rinse it immediately with clean water. Before attempting to clean an important area, practice in some less conspicuous place. Test-clean to make certain the cleaner doesn't discolor the bricks.

SAWTOOTH EDGING

Sawtooth edging, Illus. 131, can be set up using a guide line or alongside a 2x4 or 2x6 on edge. The form can be set on top of grade or in a trench. Hold forms in place with stakes. Only excavate to depth edging requires. The starting brick should rest against undisturbed soil or be locked in position with concrete. Butt bricks edge to edge, no mortar joint.

(131)

BRICK TREE WELLS

Tree roots require air, water and minerals. When a grade is changed and the depth of soil over the roots is increased or decreased, the roots have difficulty attaining a normal amount of air, water and minerals.

If you raise a grade 6″ or less, and the soil is high in organic matter, the change won't affect most trees. When making a drastic change as shown in Illus. 132, 133, 135, you can supply what the tree needs by constructing a brick well in position shown.

Illus. 132, 133, 135, show a round tree well. Drain tile placed in position indicated around perimeter, empties water caught in well. Since the tile is placed on existing grade, it continues to provide air and water to roots.

(132)

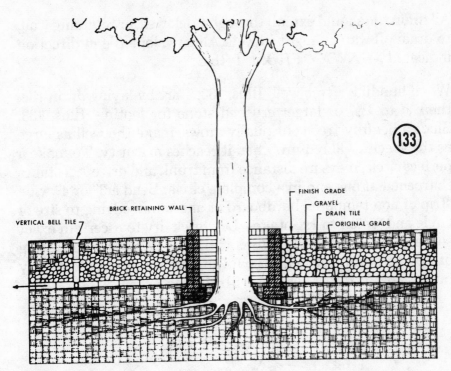

Vertical bell tiles, placed in position shown, Illus. 133, provide air and water to roots.

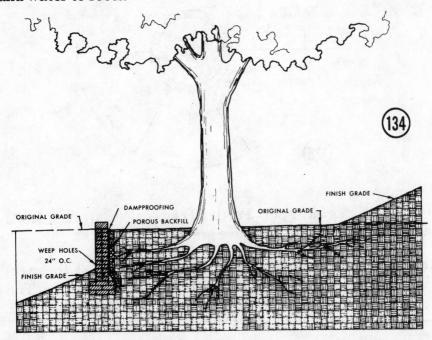

95

All drain tile should extend through brick well, or retaining wall, to drain off water caught in well. Always slope tile in direction indicated — AWAY FROM TREE.

When building a tree well, Illus. 135, start by laying drain tile, then 1″ to 1½″ or larger crushed stone for footing, Illus. 133. Since a healthy tree continually grows, make the well as large as the species will require when it reaches maturity. To make a perfect circle, measure distance from trunk and drive 1x2 stakes sharpened at one end in a complete circle. Bend a 3″ or 4″ wide strip of non tempered hardboard or aluminum edging to size of circle and fasten to 1x2 stakes. Lay brick dry to ascertain exact spacing first course will require. Use Type M mortar consisting of 1 part Portland cement, ¼ part lime to 3 parts of sand on any brick that's in direct contact with the earth.

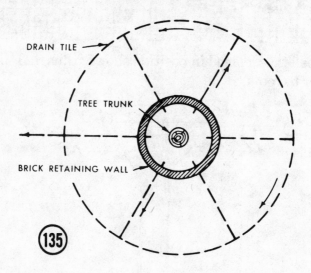

DRAIN TILE

TREE TRUNK

BRICK RETAINING WALL

(135)

Use Type S mortar, 1 part Portland cement, ½ part lime to 4½ parts sand for brick work above grade.

Raising or lowering the grade beyond the roots of the tree, Illus. 134, with a retaining wall, has little effect on the tree. The wall should be constructed so that footings go down below frost level.

BRICK HOUSES — NEW CONSTRUCTION

Since early Colonial days, brick houses have always been held in high esteem. Today, because of their resale value, lower maintenance costs, recognized charm and ability to withstand the rigors of surburban small fry, a brick house has even greater appeal.

Most building codes now accept a 6″ load bearing brick wall, Illus. 136. While these can be laid up on 6″ foundations, many codes still specify a minimum 8″ or 10″ foundation. You can meet code requirements by laying a 10″ wide course of brick, on an 8″ foundation up to floor joists, Illus. 137.

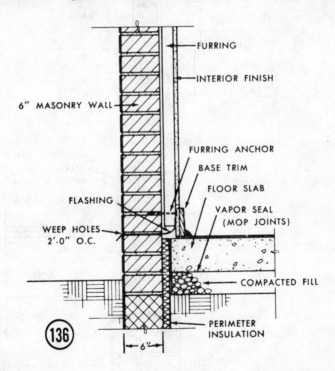

6″ MASONRY WALL

FURRING

INTERIOR FINISH

FURRING ANCHOR

BASE TRIM

FLOOR SLAB

FLASHING

VAPOR SEAL
(MOP JOINTS)

WEEP HOLES
2'-0″ O.C.

COMPACTED FILL

PERIMETER
INSULATION

(136)

6″

Or build a 10″ wide foundation and make it even easier, Illus. 138. The 6″ brick is backed up with a 4″ course to provide a nominal 10″ thick wall.

Metal ties, Illus. 137, should be placed in courses not more than 16″ apart. Use the Z tie, Illus. 95, 139.

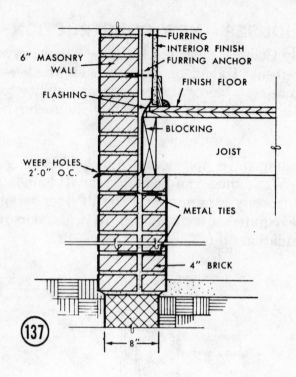

FURRING
INTERIOR FINISH
6" MASONRY WALL
FURRING ANCHOR
FINISH FLOOR
FLASHING
BLOCKING
JOIST
WEEP HOLES 2'-0" O.C.
METAL TIES
4" BRICK
137
8"

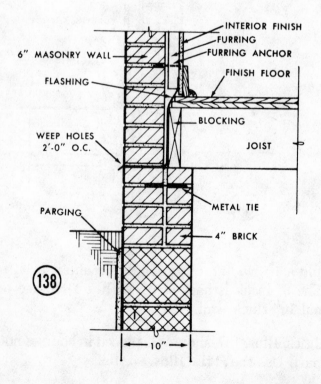

INTERIOR FINISH
FURRING
6" MASONRY WALL
FURRING ANCHOR
FINISH FLOOR
FLASHING
BLOCKING
JOIST
WEEP HOLES 2'-0" O.C.
METAL TIE
PARGING
4" BRICK
138
10"

As you build wall up to floor joist level, place metal Z ties, Illus. 139, every 36″ in first course below joists.

To make fire cuts, specified by most codes, cut ends of floor joists to angle shown, Illus. 139, and by dash lines in Illus. 140.

Nail metal anchors to ends of every fourth joist, Illus. 139. Space and nail solid bridging between joists at 8′ intervals. Nail metal anchors not further than 8′ on centers where lateral support is required or in position local codes require.

Lay up brick between floor joists, Illus. 140, level with top edge of joists.

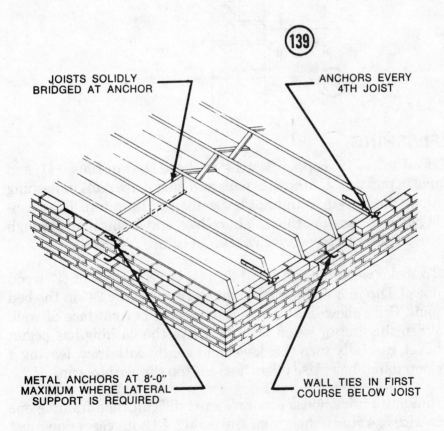

(139)

JOISTS SOLIDLY
BRIDGED AT ANCHOR

ANCHORS EVERY
4TH JOIST

METAL ANCHORS AT 8′-0″
MAXIMUM WHERE LATERAL
SUPPORT IS REQUIRED

WALL TIES IN FIRST
COURSE BELOW JOIST

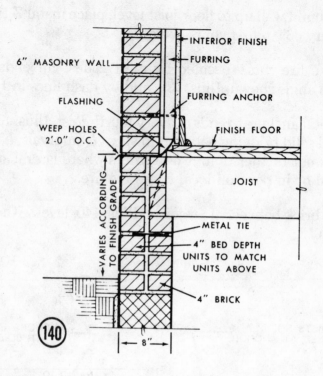

6" MASONRY WALL

INTERIOR FINISH

FURRING

FLASHING

FURRING ANCHOR

WEEP HOLES
2'-0" O.C.

FINISH FLOOR

VARIES ACCORDING
TO FINISH GRADE

JOIST

METAL TIE

4" BED DEPTH
UNITS TO MATCH
UNITS ABOVE

4" BRICK

(140)

8"

FLASHING

Bend 16" to 18" copper flashing to shape shown, Illus. 141, and nail in position. Use copper nails and only drive nails in flashing along the top edge, and not lower than 1" from top. The flashing diverts moisture that might collect, and drains it off through weep holes placed every two feet, in course indicated.

To make weep holes, Illus. 140, 141, cut 8" pieces of ⅜" wood dowel. Dip in used motor oil and place one every 24" in the bed joint. Only allow end of dowel to project beyond face of wall. When the first or second course above the flashing has begun to set, carefully turn the dowel and gently withdraw, leaving a clean round hole. Use pliers if end is too slippery to grip.

Building a brick house isn't any more difficult than framing one in with 2x4 studs, sheathing and siding. In both cases you must allow openings for doors and windows in position plans specify. The size of rough openings are specified by the manufacturer of doors and windows selected.

Walls for a brick house can be constructed with 6″ bricks, Illus. 141. Walls are built up to plate height, then framed with a plate, ceiling joists, and rafters that follow conventional framing. Most builders nail a 2x2 furring strip to floor as a sill or shoe, approximately ¾″, or thickness of a 1x2 away from inside face of brick. They nail a 1x2 to 2x6 plate, then another 2x2 as a fire stop in position shown. 2x2 are used as studs and are nailed 16″ on centers. These studs are anchored to the brick wall with 22 gauge corrugated metal furring anchors, Illus. 141, in courses spaced 2′0″ and 5′0″ above sub-flooring. These are embedded in bed joint and nailed to 2x2 studs with 8 penny common nails.

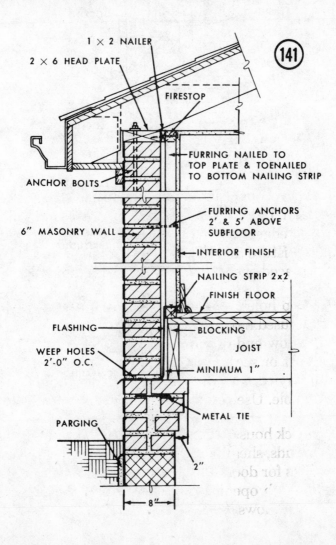

To accurately position windows, place story pole on Benchmark. Estimate number of courses needed to reach opening for a window or door. Always place the story pole at height that's equal to the benchmark, Illus. 59.

Illus. 142 shows precast door sill butting against a concrete floor slab. Note 12″ wide flashing bent to shape required to fit over metal lintel. Nail flashing to furring.

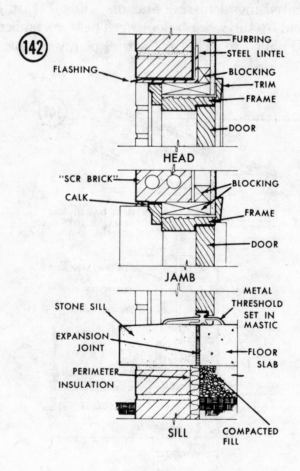

LINTELS — WINDOW, DOOR

A 6″x4″x⅜″ steel angle, Illus. 143, 144 will safely span an opening 5′4″ wide.

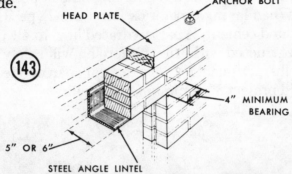

ANCHOR BOLT

HEAD PLATE

(143)

4″ MINIMUM BEARING

5″ OR 6″

STEEL ANGLE LINTEL

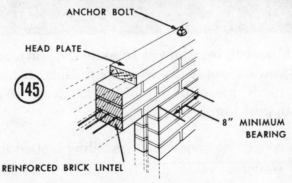

ANCHOR BOLT

HEAD PLATE

(145)

8″ MINIMUM BEARING

REINFORCED BRICK LINTEL

If you want to use a reinforced brick lintel, Illus. 145, build a 2x4 form, Illus. 146, in opening. Place on sill. Brace in level and plumb position. Use 3 No. 2 reinforcing bars in position shown, Illus. 145. When laying up a brick lintel use Type S mortar — 1 part Portland cement, ½ part hydrated lime to 4½ parts sand. A lintel constructed with this reinforcing will safely support a load of 650 lbs. per lineal foot over a clear span of 5 feet. A brick lintel should project 8″ minimum, Illus. 145.

If you use a steel lintel, allow it to extend 4″ or more beyond opening. If you have a really wide span, Illus. 144, drill holes and bolt 8″ to 10″ pieces of lintel to studs every 16″ or 32″ as needed to support lintel.

Always use copper flashing when installing a steel lintel, window or door frame.

WINDOW SILL

Illus. 147 shows one method of cutting bricks to size required to lay up a rowlock course for a sill. Always nail flashing to blocking, bend to shape shown, then lay rowlock course for sill. Most masons lay the rowlock sill under window and/or doors, after same are set and wall completed up to plate. Always provide openings to size window or door manufacturer recommends for brick construction.

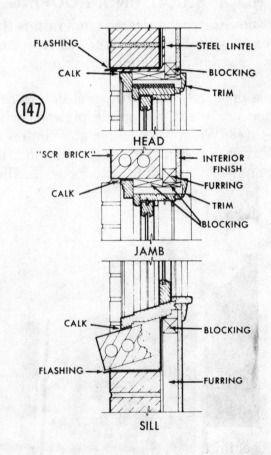

Always lay a ribbon of caulking around opening before setting window in place. Follow window manufacturers recommendations and don't skimp. This caulking provides the sealant needed to provide years of carefree service so don't substitute. Fasten window in position with fasteners manufacturer recommends.

PLATES

When a brick wall has been constructed to within 7 courses from top, 3″x6″x¼″ steel plate welded to a ½″x20″ bolts are placed in position shown, Illus. 141, 143, 144, 145. A 2x6 plate is used on a 6″ brick wall; 2x10 on a 10″ cavity wall. Anchor bolts holding plates should extend 15″ into masonry, or not less than six brick courses. Only tighten nut by hand, never with a wrench.

RAFTERS, ROOF SHEATHING, ROOFING

Most builders now use prefabricated truss rafters that are fastened to the plate with Teco fasteners. All roof sheathing and roofing follows customary building procedure.

Builders frame door openings with steel lintels, as previously explained, then use ¾ exterior grade plywood when framing opening, Illus. 148. When remodeling, steel lintels are used to support brick veneer over meter panels, air-conditioning units and other equipment fastened to exterior walls, Illus. 149.

(148)

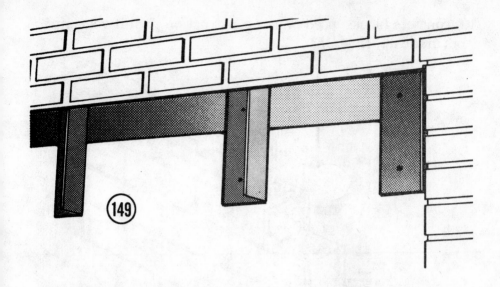

(149)

When decorative effects are desired, your masonry supply retailer will frequently cut all brick to exact angle you require,
Illus. 150. If you provide a full size pattern, he will cut brick and
number each for exact position your design requires.

(150)

10″ concrete blocks, used in new construction permit veneering from grade up, Illus. 151.

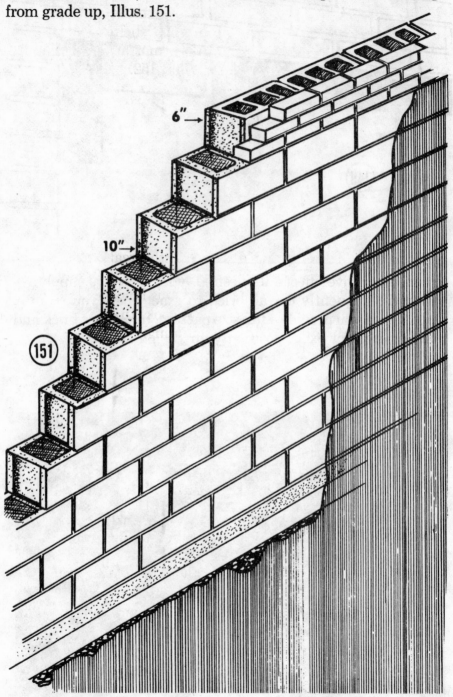

Illus. 47(6) shows a raked joint. While this is very popular for interior work, it isn't recommended for exterior walls in cold areas. The deep joints provide too much shelter for ice and snow. A raked joint is easy to do. Allow mortar to set thumbprint hard, then rake it with jointer, Illus. 152.

AN EASY TO BUILD BARBECUE

Always select location for a fireplace with great care. Do not locate it too close to trees or shrubs. Position it so prevailing winds blow toward the front opening. This helps insure a good draft and carries smoke away from the cook. In some localities, ordinances require a permit before building.

FOUNDATION — Depth and type of foundation depends upon local soil and climatic conditions. In severe frost areas, the foundation should go down below the frost line as indicated in Illus. 153. If you build in an area where no severe winters are experienced, 3½" of reinforced concrete should be sufficient.

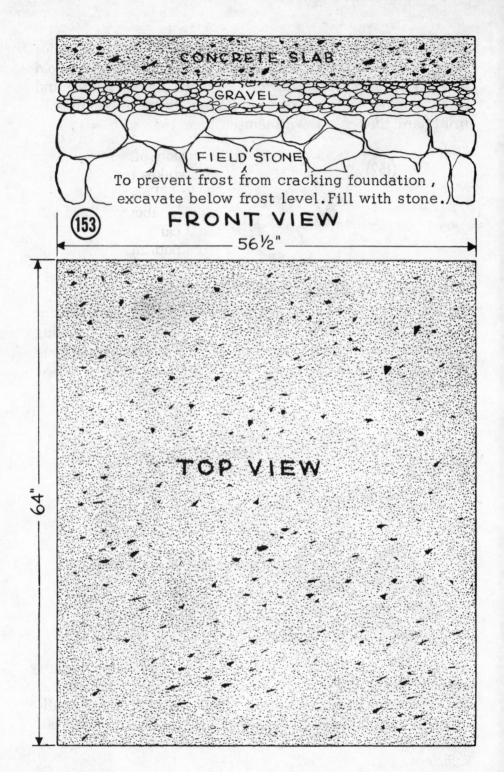

CONCRETE SLAB

GRAVEL

FIELD STONE

To prevent frost from cracking foundation,
excavate below frost level. Fill with stone.

(153) **FRONT VIEW**

56½"

TOP VIEW

64"

FROST AREAS — Dig a square cornered pit about 60″ wide, 68″ long and 12″ to 24″ deep. Fill bottom of pit with fieldstone. Work smaller stones and concrete in between fieldstones to form a solid base. Spread a 2″ layer of run-of-bank gravel on top of stones. Tamp gravel.

Build foundation form with inside dimensions of 56½″x64″, Ilus. 154. Use old lumber (2x6). Brace with stakes to hold form in place. The top edge of form should be level. This represents top of "concrete slab" and should be about 1½″ above grade. Paint inside of form with old crankcase oil so it can be easily removed after concrete has set. Wet gravel before pouring slab.

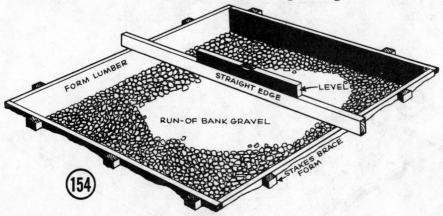

FROST FREE AREAS — Dig pit about 60″ wide, 68″ long but ONLY 3½″ deep. Build form as outlined previously. Top of form should be about 1½″ above ground level. Wet pit before pouring slab.

CONCRETE — For slab, use 1 part cement, 3 parts sand and 5 parts gravel.

Use hoe to mix concrete in tub. Lay an inch or 1½″ of concrete, then lay 6x6 reinforcing wire, Illus. 155. Complete pouring, screed level to top of form, Illus. 156. After concrete has set, (usually overnight) wet down and cover with straw or burlap. Spray it once a day for three or four days. Allow concrete to set for at least three days before starting brick work. Do not remove forms for at least 5 days. Backfill around foundation after removing forms. Do not build a fire in the fireplace during this time as the heat will draw moisture.

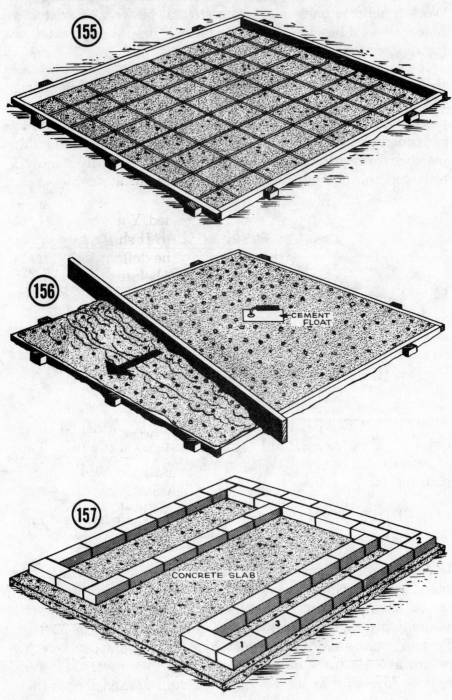

155

156

CEMENT FLOAT

157

CONCRETE SLAB

BRICKWORK — Step-by-step illustrations represent the top view of each course. Courses are numbered in the order in which they are laid. (Course 1, first — Course 2, second, etc.), Illus. 157.

A good mortar for this job consists of one part cement, 4½ parts screened sand and ½ part fireclay. Mix mortar in small batches so that it will not dry out. Dry mix 1 part cement, 4½ parts sand and ½ part fireclay or any quantity in same ratio. Add water and mix. Continue adding water and mixing until mortar is of a consistency that slips easily off the blade of hoe. If mortar begins to dry, add water. Use each batch as quickly as possible.

Brick used in fireplace should be hard-burned. You can tell hard-burned brick by striking it with a hammer. It should give off a clear, high-pitched sound in contrast to the dull thud given off by soft brick. Dip bricks in a pail of water before laying.

Start brickwork about 1″ in from side and back edges and about 4″ in from front edge of foundation. As a check, place Course No. 1 on foundation without mortar. Space bricks about ½″ apart to allow for mortar joint. Bricks should work out to overall dimensions shown in Course Illustrations.

To lay first course, spread a 1″ layer of mortar on slab where brick is to be placed. Press brick No. 1 and No. 2 in place, Illus. 157. Check with level and straight edge. Butter up end of brick No. 3 and tap into place. Check with level and straight edge. Where half-brick is indicated cut brick with chisel. Build up through Course 9, Illus. 158. Fill indicated area with broken bricks, stones, etc. This fill is designated as "rubble."

Check each course with level as work progresses. Check corners and sides with level and square to make certain they are square and plumb. Place two 3″x3″x3 ft. steel angle irons on top of ninth course of bricks as noted in Illus. 158. These angle irons support bricks across the opening. Lay Courses 10 through 19, Illus. 159.

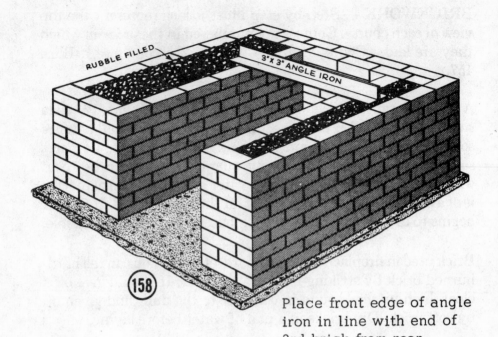

Place front edge of angle iron in line with end of 3rd brick from rear.

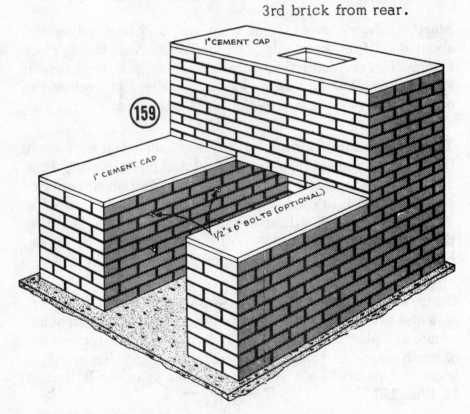

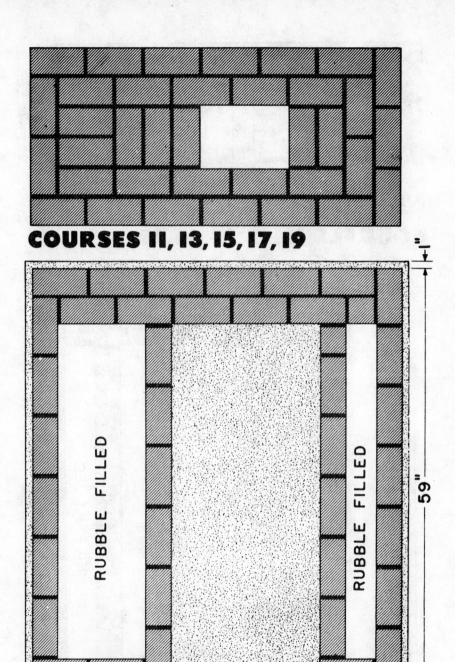

COURSES 11, 13, 15, 17, 19

RUBBLE FILLED

RUBBLE FILLED

1"

59"

4"

1" 20-1/2" 22" 12" 1"

COURSES 1, 3, 5, 7, 9

115

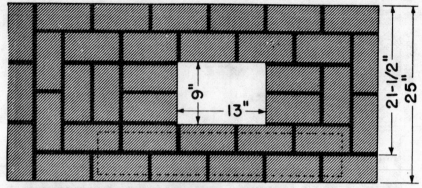

COURSES 10, 12, 14, 16, 18

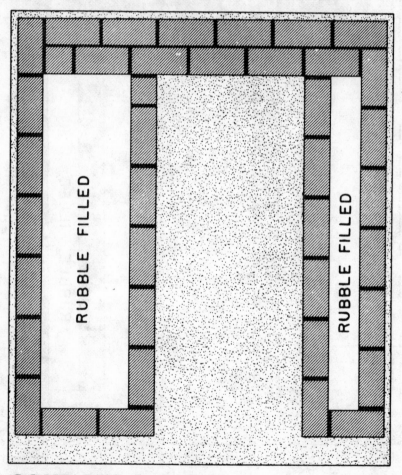

COURSES 2, 4, 6, 8

Spread a 1″ cement cap on top of chimney and top of sides. Use mortar consisting of 1 part cement to 2 parts sand. A fireplace grate 12″ x 25″ can be used across top of fireplace. A 21″ grate can be placed at any height desired. Use ½ x 6″ bolts. Embed these in concrete when setting courses, Illus. 160.

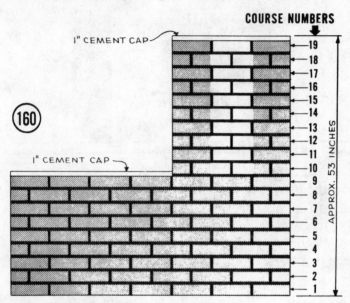

LIST OF MATERIALS
725 bricks (allows for breakage)
6 sacks cement
6 cu. ft. river sand
½ yd. fine screened sand
10 cu. ft. run-of-bank gravel
75 lbs. fireclay or lime
75 lineal ft. ½″ reinforcing rods or old 1″ pipe
Two 3″ x 3″ x 3 ft. angle irons
eight ½ x 6″ bolts (optional)

FROST AREAS: If building foundation below frost level, get 1 yd. fieldstone, 1/3 yd. gravel, 1 sack cement and 2 sacks of sand in addition to the materials listed above.

If your soil is exceptionally firm, you can pour foundation slab without building a form. If you pour without a form, dig pit with inside dimensions of 56½″ x 64″.

SUPERCHEF BARBECUE

LIST OF MATERIALS

¼ cubic yard sand
1 cubic yard gravel
Buy cement as needed
1 — 2x8x10'
1 — ¼"x8"x60" plyscord
1 — 24"x24" — ¼" or ⅜" hardware wire
1 — 34"x91" — 6x6 wire reinforcing
1 — fireplace grate — this can be 36" or 42" x 22" or 24"

FOUNDATION

Illus. 161 shows side and top view of foundation. If ground is firm, no form will be needed. Excavate area 35" x 92" by 10" to 12" deep. If you live in a cold climate, you might find it expedient to dig down 24" to 30" and fill excavation with stone to within 4" to 6" of grade level. Cover stone with gravel.

Using 1 part cement, 3 parts sand and 5 parts gravel, pour and level 2" of concrete. Lay a 34" x 91" piece of 6x6 reinforcing wire, then pour an additional 2" to 4" of concrete. Allow foundation to set at least 3 days before starting to lay brick.

If soil is sandy, a form can be built with 2x6 or 2x8's. It will be necessary to excavate area slightly larger so inside dimension of form measures 35" x 92". Keep top edge level. Use a 2x4 across top of form as a screed to level concrete.

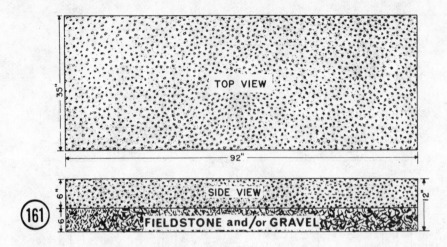

Step by step illustrations of each course represent a top view, courses are numbered in order they are laid. Start all brick work about 1″ in from edge of foundation. Lay bricks to overall dimensions noted. Spread a ½″ layer of mortar on foundation for starting Course No. 1, Illus. 162. Course No. 2 is shown in Illus. 163. After laying Course No. 3, start filling in area marked "rubble" with broken brick or fieldstone and concrete.

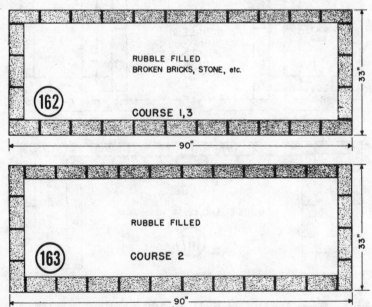

Proceed to build up through Course 14, Illus. 167. Check each course with a level. Check corners with a square.

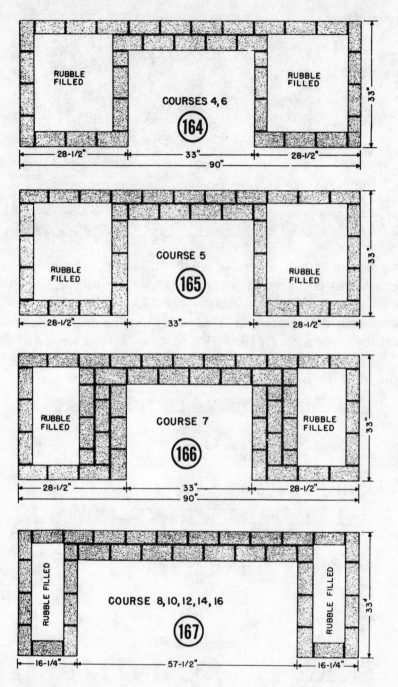

RUBBLE FILLED

RUBBLE FILLED

COURSES 4, 6

(164)

28-1/2" — 33" — 28-1/2"

90"

33"

RUBBLE FILLED

RUBBLE FILLED

COURSE 5

(165)

28-1/2" — 33" — 28-1/2"

33"

RUBBLE FILLED

RUBBLE FILLED

COURSE 7

(166)

28-1/2" — 33" — 28-1/2"

90"

33"

RUBBLE FILLED

RUBBLE FILLED

COURSE 8, 10, 12, 14, 16

(167)

16-1/4" — 57-1/2" — 16-1/4"

33"

To build a form for the arch, Illus. 168, use 2x8 and ¼″ plyscord. Illus. 169 shows angle of arch. Cut two 2x8 to length indicated. Nail plyscord to 2x8 with 8 penny common nails.

120

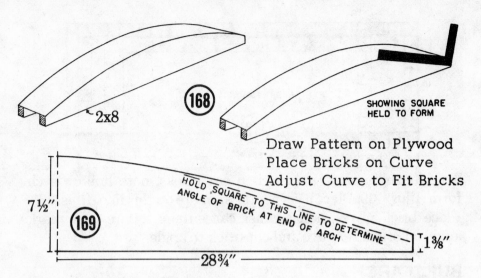

168

2x8

SHOWING SQUARE
HELD TO FORM

Draw Pattern on Plywood
Place Bricks on Curve
Adjust Curve to Fit Bricks

7½″

169

HOLD SQUARE TO THIS LINE TO DETERMINE
ANGLE OF BRICK AT END OF ARCH

1⅜″

28¾″

Illus. 170 shows arch in place.

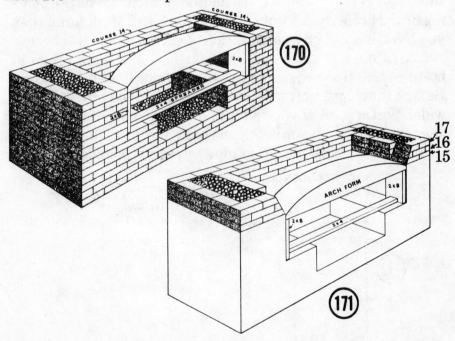

COURSE 14

COURSE 14

170

2x8

2x4 SPREADER

2x8

17
16
15

ARCH FORM

2x8

2x8

2x4

171

Cut 2x8 legs to height required to support form in position shown. Keep form flush with outside face of fireplace. Use a 2x4 spreader as shown.

Cut end bricks for courses 15, 16, 17, to bevel shown, Illus. 171. Lay Courses 15, 16, 17, Illus. 172, 167.

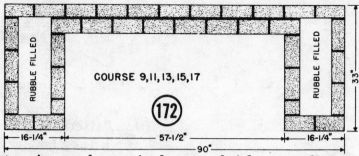

To determine angle required to cut bricks, note line on arch form, Illus. 169. Place a carpenter's square on this line, Illus. 168. Place brick in position against carpenter's square, and mark angle on brick. Remove and cut brick to angle.

BUILD ARCH

Illus. 170, 171, 173 shows construction of arch. To insure spacing bricks properly, lay out bricks on the form. Mark form when you have established exact position of each brick. It will be necessary to use a slightly wider mortar joint at the top than at bottom. Lay front course of bricks on arch, then back course. Be sure to stagger mortar joints. This can be done with a slightly wider mortar joint or you can split a brick in half edgewise for a starting brick at one or both ends of arch, Illus. 173. Take particular care to make mortar joints as strong as possible.

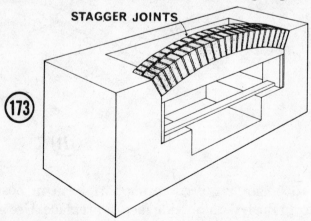

When you have completed laying bricks for arch, lay front corners of Courses 18, 19, 20, Illus. 174, 175, 176, 177, Use a guide line to make certain courses are straight. Check each course

with a level. Fill in Courses 18, 19 with rubble as shown. Lay Course
No. 20, Illus. 177.

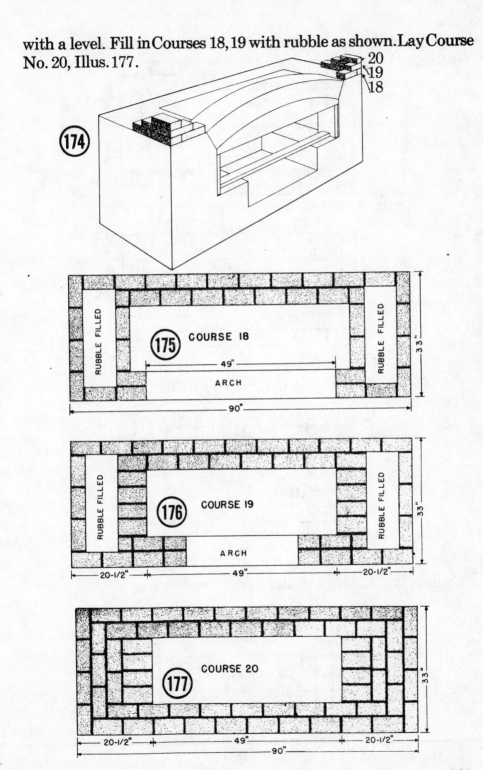

Lay Course 21, and Course 22 Illus. 178, 179, 12¼″ from edge as shown.

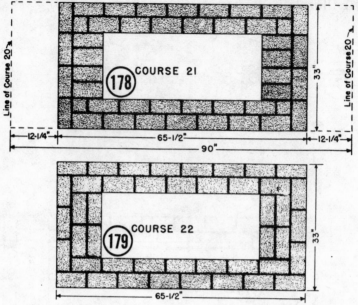

Step Course No. 23, Illus. 180, 2″ in from Course No. 22.

Course No. 24, Illus. 181, steps back another 2″.

Course No. 25, Illus. 182; Course No. 26, Illus. 183; Course No. 27, Illus. 184; Course No. 28, Illus. 185 , are all stepped back distance indicated, as are Courses 29 through to 31, Illus. 186 to 188.

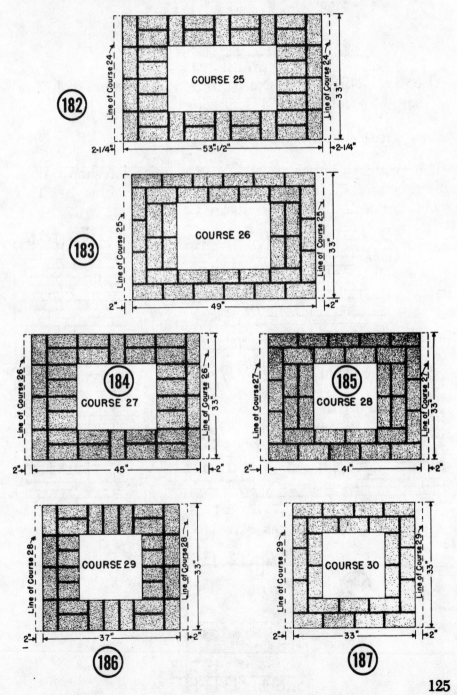

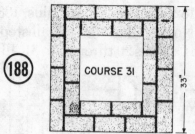

(188) COURSE 31

33"

After completing Course No. 31, Illus. 188, cut a piece of ¼″ or ⅜″ hardware cloth, 24″ x 24″ for a screen.

Place screen on top of Course 31.

Three courses of brick are laid flatwise in position shown, Illus. 189, and on ends, in between, for top Course 32, Illus. 190. This course projects 2¼″ beyond edge of Course No. 31.

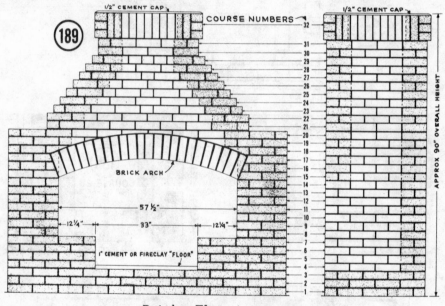

(189) ½″ CEMENT CAP   ½″ CEMENT CAP

COURSE NUMBERS — 32
31
30
29
28
27
26
25
24
23
22
21
20
19
18
BRICK ARCH
17
16
15
14
13
12
57 ½″
11
12¼″   33″   12¼″   10
9
8
7
6
1″ CEMENT OR FIRECLAY "FLOOR"   5
4
3
2
1

APPROX 90″ OVERALL HEIGHT

Bricks Flatwise   2 1/4″
Course 32   Course 31

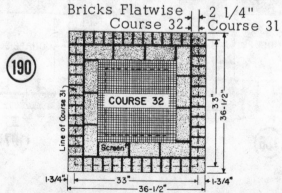

(190) COURSE 32
Line of Course 31
Screen
33"
36-1/2"
1-3/4″   33″   1-3/4″
36-1/2″

126

To support Course 32 in position, place a 2x2 collar around Course No. 31. Allow Course No. 31 to set at least 3 days before carefully putting 2x2's in position, Illus. 191. Don't drive nails into the 2x2's. Predrill holes and use 2" No. 12 flathead wood screws. Position the form gently in place. Don't jar any bricks loose. You can then lay Course No. 32 in position.

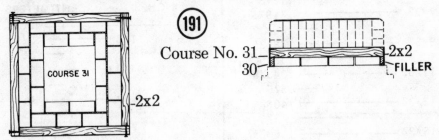

After setting Course 32, spread a ½" cement cap on top.

After Course No. 32 has been allowed to set about a week, remove the 2x2 form.

Spread a 1" layer of mortar on top of rubble at Course No. 3 for floor. Your building material dealer can supply fire clay for use on the floor, or you can lay a course of fire brick. A 36" x 24" fireplace grate can be placed on the ledge provided by Course No. 7. Grate can be raised by placing additional bricks under it, or you can insert bolts in mortar course at whatever height you wish to position the grate.

The essentials for good brick and tile construction simply stated are:

● Choose a mortar suited for the use for which the structure is designed.

● Mix mortar with as much water as possible and avoid oversanding.

● Completely fill all joints with mortar, particularly the head joints.

● Install flashing properly as required and provide weep holes for drainage.

● Protect masonry during construction with canvas or waterproof paper. Planks alone are never adequate.

EASY-TO-USE-METRIC SCALE

DECIMAL EQUIVALENTS

1/32		.03125
	1/16	.0625
3/32		.09375
	1/8	.125
5/32		.15625
	3/16	.1875
7/32		.21875
	1/4	.250
9/32		.28125
	5/16	.3125
11/32		.34375
	3/8	.375
13/32		.40625
	7/16	.4375
15/32		.46875
	1/2	.500
17/32		.53125
	9/16	.5625
19/32		.59375
	5/8	.625
21/32		.65625
	11/16	.6875
23/32		.71875
	3/4	.750
25/32		.78125
	13/16	.8125
27/32		.84375
	7/8	.875
29/32		.90625
	15/16	.9375
31/32		.96875

FRACTIONS — CENTIMETERS

1/16		0.16
	1/8	0.32
3/16		0.48
	1/4	0.64
5/16		0.79
	3/8	0.95
7/16		1.11
	1/2	1.27
9/16		1.43
	5/8	1.59
11/16		1.75
	3/4	1.91

13/16		2.06
	7/8	2.22
15/16		2.38

INCHES — CENTIMETERS

1		2.54
	1/8	2.9
	1/4	3.2
	3/8	3.5
	1/2	3.8
	5/8	4.1
	3/4	4.4
	7/8	4.8
2		5.1
	1/8	5.4
	1/4	5.7
	3/8	6.0
	1/2	6.4
	5/8	6.7
	3/4	7.0
	7/8	7.3
3		7.6
	1/8	7.9
	1/4	8.3
	3/8	8.6
	1/2	8.9
	5/8	9.2
	3/4	9.5
	7/8	9.8
4		10.2
	1/8	10.5
	1/4	10.8
	3/8	11.1
	1/2	11.4
	5/8	11.7
	3/4	12.1
	7/8	12.4
5		12.7
	1/8	13.0
	1/4	13.3
	3/8	13.7
	1/2	14.0
	5/8	14.3
	3/4	14.6
	7/8	14.9

	cm			cm
6	15.2	12		30.5
1/8	15.6	1/8		30.8
1/4	15.9	1/4		31.1
3/8	16.2	3/8		31.4
1/2	16.5	1/2		31.8
5/8	16.8	5/8		32.1
3/4	17.1	3/4		32.4
7/8	17.5	7/8		32.7
7	17.8	14		35.6
1/8	18.1	16		40.6
1/4	18.4	20		50.8
3/8	18.7	30		76.2
1/2	19.1	40		101.6
5/8	19.4	50		127.0
3/4	19.7	60		152.4
7/8	20.0	70		177.8
8	20.3	80		203.2
1/8	20.6	90		228.6
1/4	21.0	100		254.0
3/8	21.3			
1/2	21.6			
5/8	21.9			
3/4	22.2			
7/8	22.5			
9	22.9			
1/8	23.2			
1/4	23.5			
3/8	23.8			
1/2	24.1			
5/8	24.4			
3/4	24.8			
7/8	25.1			
10	25.4			
1/8	25.7			
1/4	26.0			
3/8	26.4			
1/2	26.7			
5/8	27.0			
3/4	27.3			
7/8	27.6			
11	27.9			
1/8	28.3			
1/4	28.6			
3/8	28.9			
1/2	29.2			
5/8	29.5			
3/4	29.8			
7/8	30.2			

FEET —	INCHES —	CENTIMETERS
1	12	30.5
2	24	61.0
3	36	91.4
4	48	121.9
5	60	152.4
6	72	182.9
7	84	213.4
8	96	243.8
9	108	274.3
10	120	304.8
11	132	335.3
12	144	365.8
13	156	396.2
14	168	426.7
15	180	457.2
16	192	487.7
17	204	518.2
18	216	548.6
19	228	579.1
20	240	609.6

HOW TO USE A LEVEL, LEVEL-TRANSIT

Every building, masonry, grading, driveway, and drainage job, to mention but a few, requires establishing accurate layout lines as described on page 48. All construction requires level and plumb lines. Guide lines must be straight, level, corners square and plumb.

Just as a carpenter's square, Illus. 55, helps establish a right angle, so a level, Illus. 192, a level-transit, Illus. 193, or a hand held Sight Level, Illus. 194, assist in sighting and establishing straight level lines and/or planes.

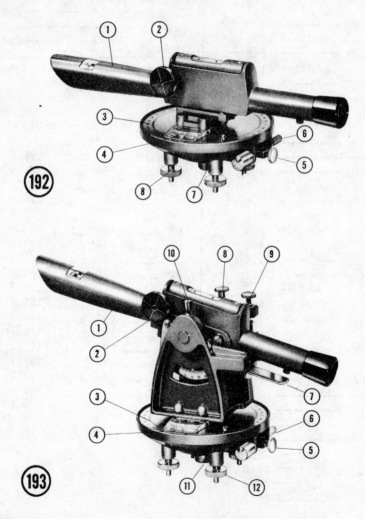

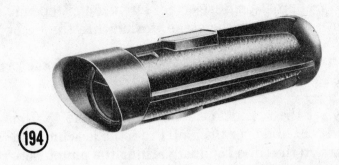

Guide lines that are square, level, or pitch to grade job requires, are easy to establish, and are a must for every construction job. You can set up guide lines in a number of different ways. The accepted way is to select one corner of the proposed site, and drive a stake, Illus. 66, as explained on page 48.

To stake out a site, erect batter boards, check footings, foundation forms, or lay out a terrace with the proper angle of slope to provide drainage, use a level, level-transit, or a sight level.

You can lay out guide lines for a small area using a straight edged 2x4 or 2x6 and a level, Illus. 82. To establish guide lines like a pro, borrow or rent a level, level-transit, or a True Sight Level.

ESTABLISH ACCURATE GUIDE LINES

During the earliest days of civilized man, some smarty figured out that the most accurate distant measurement required a perfectly straight line of sight. Today's modern level, and level-transit works on the same basic principle. Since a line of sight is a perfectly straight line, every point along the line is level with all other points on that line. If you are building a wall, and want to make certain the guide lines, footing forms, or any course is level, set up a level-transit and check the wall at various points.

When starting any job, measure the exact distance from house, or property line, to one corner of the project. Drive a stake flush into the ground at point selected. Drive a 4 or 6 penny nail, or tack, into the top of the stake, to indicate the exact corner.

To set up a level, or level-transit, spread the tripod legs at least 36 inches.

Visually set the tripod so the horizontal circle #3, Illus. 192, is level and centered over the nail. Press the legs into the earth to make certain the tripod is steady. Hang the plumb bob from the tripod so point of bob is centered directly over nail, Illus. 195.

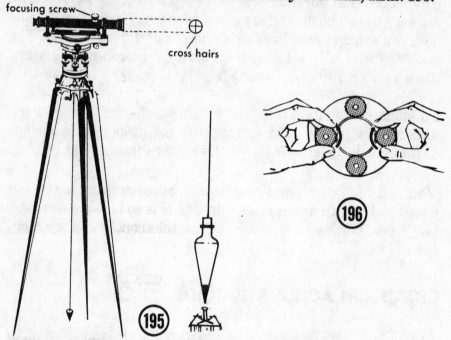

focusing screw

cross hairs

(196)

(195)

After leveling the instrument as much as the tripod allows, start to "fine tune" by turning the leveling screws #8, Illus. 192, 196.

To fully appreciate how a level, Illus. 192; or a level-transit, Illus. 193 functions, note the various adjustments. The telescope itself is a precision made sighting device with a carefully ground and polished lens that produces a clear, sharp, magnified image. The magnification of a telescope is described as its "power." An 18 power telescope will make a distant object appear 18 times closer than when viewed with the naked eye. Cross hairs in telescope permit the object sighted to be centered exactly.

132

The leveling vial, Illus. 197, also called a bubble, works like any familiar carpenter's level, but on the level-transit it is more sensitive and more accurately mounted. Four leveling screws, No. 8, Illus. 192, permit leveling the vial perfectly.

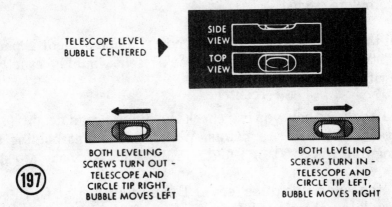

TELESCOPE LEVEL
BUBBLE CENTERED

SIDE VIEW

TOP VIEW

(197)

BOTH LEVELING SCREWS TURN OUT - TELESCOPE AND CIRCLE TIP RIGHT, BUBBLE MOVES LEFT

BOTH LEVELING SCREWS TURN IN - TELESCOPE AND CIRCLE TIP LEFT, BUBBLE MOVES RIGHT

To level the telescope, place it in position on tripod, over two leveling screws, Illus. 198. Grasp both leveling screws, Illus. 196, between the thumb and forefinger, and turn them so as to loosen one and tighten the other at the same time. This is done by turning the wheels either towards each other, or away from each other according to which way the bubble is to be moved. When you center the bubble in the vial, the telescope is level in that direction.

(198)

Now turn the telescope at right angles (90°), and center it over the other pair of leveling screws. When level in this direction it is considered level in both directions. Don't tighten the leveling screws too tight, or leave them too loose. If loose, errors will occur, if too tight, the instrument will be strained.

If leveling the instrument has thrown the point of bob off the tack, correct the position of the instrument. Again check to make certain it's level. To focus, turn knob #2, Illus. 192.

The circle, Illus. 192, is merely a flat plate on which the telescope rotates. It is marked in degrees so the telescope can be rotated in any horizontal direction, and any horizontal angle can be quickly measured on this circle. Most level-transits have a vernier scale, #4, Illus. 192, which divides each degree into minutes for accuracy. There are 60 minutes in each degree — 360° in a complete circle.

When the instrument is level, we know the line of sight is perfectly straight. Any point on the line of sight would be exactly level with any other point.

Illus. 199, shows how you can check the difference in height (or elevation) between two points. With an assistant holding a leveling rod, Illus. 200, or a folding rule, Illus. 53, make a test.

When the rule reads three feet at B, and four feet at C, Illus. 199, you know there's a difference of one foot. Using the same principle, you can easily check to see if a footing form is level; if concrete blocks, a course of brick, windows, or doors are in line. You can also see how much a driveway slopes.

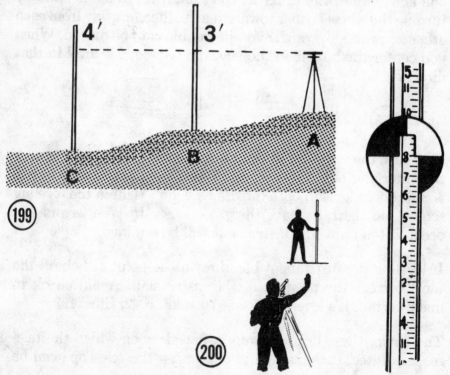

If you decide to purchase a level-transit, be sure to obtain one with the zoom lens and the magnification you need for the type of work you plan on doing.

When sighting through the telescope, keep both eyes open. You will find this eliminates squinting, doesn't tire the eyes, and gives the best view through the telescope.

To establish the difference in grade between several points, do this. Set the instrument about midway between two points. Level the instrument as previously explained. Hold the rod straight up at X. Read the telescope, Illus. 201. When the horizontal cross hair lens cuts the graduations on the rod, note the reading. Place rod at Y. Without disturbing the instrument, swing the telescope clear around, sight rod, note reading. The difference between the two will tell how much one station is above or below the other. If X reads 4'2" and Y reads 2'8", station X is 1'6" below station Y.

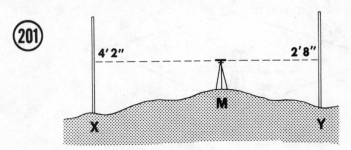

If you can see all points of the area to be surveyed, i.e., Illus. 201, proceed as suggested. If you have a situation where you must establish grades over a rise, Illus. 202, start at C, and work your way over the hill. Do section 1, 2, 3, etc.

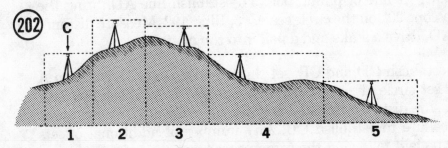

To lay out a site for an addition, garage, or other building, measure the required distance from the house or property line, and drive a 2x2 stake to indicate one corner flush into the ground. Drive a tack or 4 penny nail into the stake. The nail now represents the exact corner. Place tripod in position making certain it's pressed firmly into ground. If you are working on a paved surface, be sure the points on tripod are spread 3½'. Center plumb bob directly over the nail.

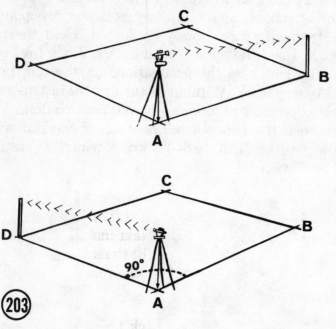

Focus along line AB to establish the front or one side of the building, Illus. 203. Using a steel tape, measure exact distance required, drive a stake, and a nail into top of stake at exact corner. To double check position of nail, hold a plumb bob over the nail. Sight line of plumb bob. To establish line AD, bring the telescope 90° on the circle scale, #3, Illus. 192. Measure distance of AD, drive a stake and a nail into top of stake.

To establish CD and CB, set the tripod up over D. Sight to A and set circle at zero. Turn telescope 90° to establish line DC. Measure distance required and drive a stake at C. Follow same procedure to establish CB. Any number of additional offsets can be laid following the same procedure.

The plumb bob over nail not only indicates a corner, but also the zero point of each angle. To establish corners on an odd shaped site, Illus. 204, set the instrument up at station 1, level it as explained previously, swing the telescope to establish station 2.

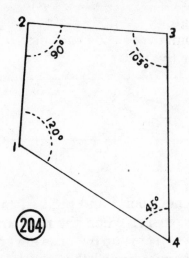

(204)

Set the horizontal circle and the vernier guide, #4, Illus 192, at zero. Then turn the telescope to sight on station 4 and read the angle. In this case it would read 120°. Next move the tripod to station 2. Level up as suggested, and sight to read station 1. Set the horizontal circle at zero, then sight the telescope to locate station 3, and read the angle 90°.

Place instrument on station 3, sight back to station 2. Set the circle at zero. Turn the telescope to sight station 4. Your angle should be 105°. The same procedure is followed to measure or double check angle at station 4.

Double check the correctness of your readings by adding the four inside angles. The total of the inside angles of the quadrangle is always 360°.

To lay out any angle proceed in the same way. Set the instrument at station 1, and set the circle at zero. Swing the telescope to the desired angle. Place the rod in position so that it intersects the vertical cross hairs. Drive a stake. One leg of an angle is thus established.

RUNNING STRAIGHT LINES WITH A LEVEL

Level the instrument over the first point, Illus. 205. Hold the rod at the first stake point and adjust the position of the target so it falls on the cross hairs of the instrument. Make a note of the height.

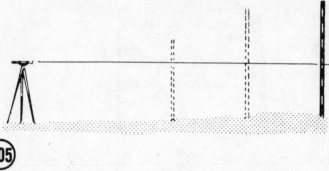

(205)

Move the rod to the next point and proceed as before. Repeat as many times as necessary. When the rod moves beyond the range of the instrument, set it up over the next to the last mark point. Focus the instrument until the target falls in the cross hairs. Proceed as before. This is an invaluable aid in setting up fencing so the top rail is level all the way through.

ESTABLISH VERTICAL LINES AND PLANES

To establish vertical lines and planes, use a level-transit. Level the instrument as previously described, then release the locking levers which hold the telescope in level position. Swing the telescope vertically and horizontally until the line to be established is directly on the vertical cross hair. If the telescope is now rotated up or down, Illus. 206, each point cut by the vertical cross hair is in a vertical plane with the starting point.

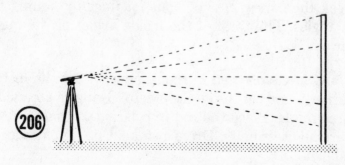

(206)

SIGHT LEVEL

A Sight Level, Illus. 194, is a carefully made precision instrument designed to simplify many jobs. It has a spirit level and cross hair that indicates true level of sight. It was developed using the same principle of operation as a surveying instrument.

Hold the Sight Level with either hand, being careful not to cover the level vial located at the top of the level. The sensitive level vial, the cross hair, and the object on which you are sighting, can all be seen through the level at the same time. To obtain a true level line of sight, sight through the slotted eyepiece and raise or lower the large end slightly until the vial is level and centered with the cross hair. A level line of sight is a continuous, perfectly straight line, for as far as you can see. All points and objects along this line are exactly level with your eye.

The Sight Level permits accurately checking the level of retaining walls, fences, masonry, batter boards, foundations, etc., by simply sighting on the object and noting its position in relation to the level line of sight through the level. To establish or determine differences in level, an assistant holds a measuring rod or folding rule and notes measurements.

Sight through the level, with vial bubble centered. Have your assistant note or mark off measurements on the rod. For example, the first reading at A, Illus. 207, is 4'. Have rod moved to location B. Without moving your position take another reading. If the reading on the rod at B is 5 feet, the difference in elevation between the two points is one foot.

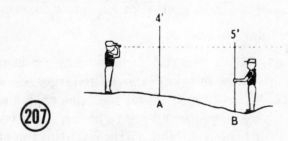

HOW TO ESTABLISH SLOPE OR PITCH

If you want to lay a drain or grade a surface and want, for example, a pitch of ¼″ per foot, and the end point is 16′, place the measuring rod on selected point and take a reading. If point A, Illus. 208, reads 5′0″ and you want a reading of 5′4″ at B, excavate to depth requires.

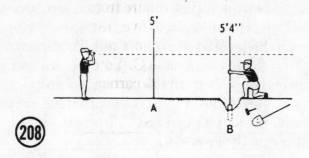

This establishes a 4″ pitch in 16′0″ and tells you where and how deep to dig. For more accurate readings over long distance, steady the Sight Level against a board rested on any solid object.

TO LAY OUT A BUILDING
AND SET UP BATTER BOARDS

To set up batter boards, Illus. 67, so the top edge is level with all other batter boards, follow this procedure.

Set the transit in the middle of the building site, and level as previously outlined. Decide what height masonry is to be laid, and drive a stake. Use length needed. Drive a nail to establish a grade mark, at point above grade chosen for the completed foundation.

Position bottom edge of target rod so it touches grade mark. Move the rod to next stake but don't move the target. Hold rod against next stake. When line in target matches cross hair on lens, mark stake. Drive two more stakes to indicate one corner. Check each stake with the rod. Nail batter board to the stakes so top edge of batter board is at height of the original guide mark.

Drive stakes and nail batter boards at the same level at all corners. When all batter boards check level, drive a nail into top edge of batter board to establish location for building lines. Set the transit over stake A and level it. Sight toward B. Using a plumb bob to guide you, drive a nail into batter board. Measure from A to B and drive a stake to indicate exact corner of B. Set a nail in stake to indicate the exact corner. Now sight toward J and put a nail into batter board. Measure from A to C and drive a stake and a nail into top of stake. Move transit to B and level it. Sight towards D. Measure and drive a nail. A line stretched from A to C marks the front line A C. You can tie pieces of string, Illus. 209, 67, to indicate exact corner.

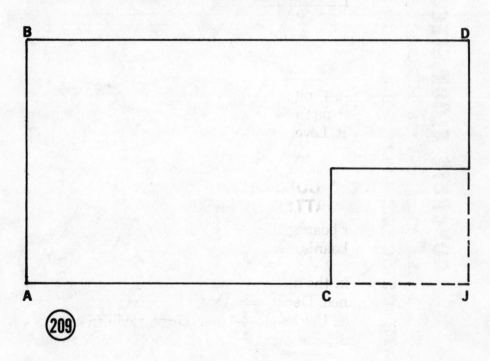

(209)

CONCRETE BLOCK SIZES

A– 7 5/8"   B– 15 5/8"   C–9 5/8"   D– 11 5/8"   E– 3 5/8"

APPROXIMATE METRIC SIZE   A-19.37   B-39.7   C-24.45   D-29.53   E-9.21

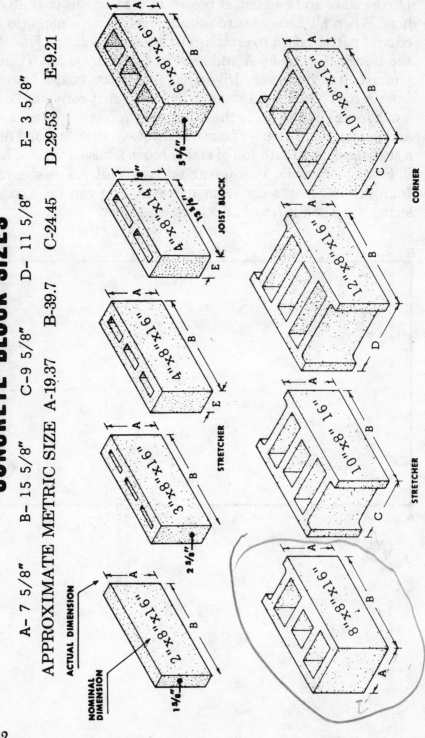

6"x8"x16"

10"x8"x16"

CORNER

5 5/8"

4"x8"x14"

JOIST BLOCK

E

12"x8"x16"

4"x8"x16"

STRETCHER

E

3"x8"x16"

2 5/8"

D

10"x8"x16"

STRETCHER

C

2"x8"x16"

ACTUAL DIMENSION

NOMINAL DIMENSION

1 5/8"

8"x8"x16"

142

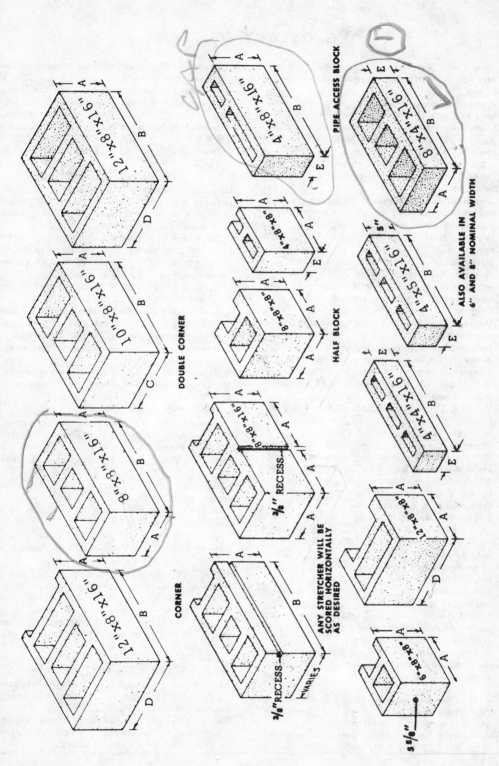

12"x8"x16"

10"x8"x16"

8"x8"x16"

12"x8"x16"

DOUBLE CORNER

CORNER

4"x8"x16"

4"x8"x8"

8"x8"x8"

HALF BLOCK

8"x8"x16"

3/8" RECESS

3/8" RECESS
VARIES

ANY STRETCHER WILL BE
SCORED HORIZONTALLY
AS DESIRED

8"x4"x16"

PIPE ACCESS BLOCK

8"x4"x16"

**ALSO AVAILABLE IN
6" AND 8" NOMINAL WIDTH**

4"x5"x16"
5"

4"x4"x16"

12"x8"x8"

6"x8"x9"
5⅝"

143

GLOSSARY OF TERMS

Admixtures: Materials added to mortar as water-repellent or coloring agents, or to retard or hasten setting.

Anchor: A piece or assemblage, usually metal, used to attach building parts (e.g., plates, joists, trusses, etc.) to masonry or masonry materials.

Arch: A curved, compressive, structural member, spanning openings or recesses; also built flat.

Back Arch: A concealed arch carrying the backing of a wall where the exterior facing is carried by a lintel.

Architectural Terra Cotta: Hard-burned, glazed or unglazed clay building units, plain or ornamental, machine-extruded or hand-molded, and generally larger in size than brick or facing tile. See *Ceramic Veneer*.

Back Filling: 1. Rough masonry built behind a facing or between two faces. 2. Filling over the extrados of an arch. 3. Brickwork in spaces between structural timbers, sometimes called *brick nogging*.

Backup: That part of a masonry wall behind the exterior facing.

Bat: A piece of brick.

Batter: Recessing or sloping masonry back in successive courses; the opposite of corbel.

Bed Joint: The horizontal layer of mortar on which a masonry unit is laid.

Bond: 1. Tying various parts of a masonry wall together by lapping units one over another or by connecting with metal ties. 2. Patterns formed by exposed faces of units. 3. Adhesion between mortar or grout and masonry units or reinforcement.

Bond Course: The course consisting of units which overlap more than one wythe of masonry.

Brick: A solid masonry unit of clay or shale, formed into a rectangular prism while plastic and burned or fired in a kiln.

Acid-Resistant Brick: Brick suitable for use in contact with chemicals, usually in conjunction with acid-resistant mortars.

Adobe Brick: Large roughly-molded, sun-dried clay brick of varying sizes.

Angle Brick: Any brick shaped to an oblique angle to fit a salient corner.

Arch Brick: 1. Wedge-shaped brick for special use in an arch. 2. Extremely hard-burned brick from an arch of a scove kiln.

Building Brick: Brick for building purposes not especially treated for texture or color. Formerly called *common brick*. See ASTM Specifications C 62.

Dry-Press Brick: Brick formed in molds under high pressures from relatively dry clay (5 to 7 per cent moisture content).

Economy Brick: Brick whose nominal dimensions are 4 by 4 by 8 in.

Engineered Brick: Brick whose nominal dimensions are 3⅕ by 4 by 8 in.

Facing Brick: Brick made especially for facing purposes, often treated to produce surface texture. They are made of selected clays, or treated, to produce desired color. See ASTM Specifications C 216.

Fire Brick: Brick made of refractory ceramic material which will resist high temperatures.

Floor Brick: Smooth dense brick, highly resistant to abrasion, used as finished floor surfaces.

Gaged Brick: 1. Brick which have been ground or otherwise produced to accurate dimensions. 2. A tapered arch brick.

Jumbo Brick: A generic term indicating a brick larger in size than the standard. Some producers use this term to describe oversize brick of specific dimensions manufactured by them.

Norman Brick: A brick whose nominal dimensions are 2⅔ by 4 by 12 in.

Paving Brick: Vitrified brick especially suitable for use in pavements where resistance to abrasion is important. See ASTM Specifications C 7.

Roman Brick: Brick whose nominal dimensions are 2 by 4 by 12 in.

Salmon Brick: Relatively soft; under-burned brick, so named because of color. Sometimes called *chuff* or *place* brick.

"SCR brick"[1]: See SCR.

Sewer Brick: Low absorption, abrasive-resistant brick intended for use in drainage structures. See ASTM Specifications C 32.

Buttering: Placing mortar on a masonry unit with a trowel.

Chase: A continuous recess built into a wall to receive pipes, ducts, etc.

Clay Mortar-Mix: Finely ground clay used as a plasticizer for masonry mortars.

Clip: A portion of a brick cut to length.

Closer: The last brick or tile laid in a course. It may be whole or a portion of a unit.

Coping: The material or masonry units forming a cap or finish on top of a wall, pier, pilaster, chimney, etc. It protects masonry below from penetration of water from above.

Corbel: A shelf or ledge formed by projecting successive courses of masonry out from the face of the wall.

Course: One of the continuous horizontal layers of units, bonded with mortar, in masonry.

Efflorescence: A powder or stain sometimes found on the surface of masonry, resulting from deposition of water-soluble salts.

Face: 1. The exposed surface of a wall or masonry unit. 2. The surface of a unit designed to be exposed in the finished masonry.

144

Facing: Any material, forming a part of a wall, used as a finished surface.

Flashing: A thin impervious material placed in mortar joints and through air spaces in masonry to prevent water penetration and/or provide water drainage.

Furring: A method of finishing the interior face of a masonry wall to provide space for insulation, prevent moisture transmittance, or to provide a level surface for finishing.

Grounds: Nailing strips placed in masonry walls as a means of attaching trim or furring.

Grout: A cementitious component of high-water-cement ratio, permitting it to be poured into spaces within masonry walls. Grout consists of portland cement, lime and aggregate. It is often formed by adding water to mortar.

Hard-Burned: Nearly vitrified clay products which have been fired at high temperatures. They have relatively low absorptions and high compressive strengths.

Head Joint: The vertical mortar joint between ends of masonry units. Often called *cross joint*.

Header: A masonry unit which overlaps two or more adjacent wythes of masonry to tie them together. Often called *bonder*.

Lateral Support: Means whereby walls are braced either vertically or horizontally by columns, pilasters, cross-walls, beams, floors, roofs, etc.

Lime, Hydrated: Quicklime to which sufficient water has been added to convert the oxides to hydroxides.

Lime Putty: Hydrated lime in plastic form ready for addition to mortar.

Lintel: A beam placed over an opening in a wall.

Masonry: Brick, tile, stone, etc., or combinations thereof, bonded with mortar.

Masonry Cement: A mill-mixed mortar to which sand and water must be added.

Mortar: A plastic mixture of cementitious materials, fine aggregate and water. See ASTM Specifications C 270.

Partition: An interior wall, one story or less in height.

Pargeting: The process of applying a coat of cement mortar to masonry. Often spelled and/or pronounced *parging*.

Pick and Dip: A method of laying brick whereby the bricklayer simultaneously picks up a brick with one hand and, with the other hand, enough mortar on a trowel to lay the brick. Sometimes called the *Eastern* or *New England* method.

Pier: An isolated column of masonry.

Pilaster: A wall portion projecting from either or both wall faces and serving as a vertical column and/or beam.

Pointing: Troweling mortar into a joint after masonry units are laid.

Racking: A method entailing stepping back suc-

cessive courses of masonry.

Raggle: A groove in a joint or special unit to receive roofing or flashing.

RBM: 1. Reinforced brick masonry. 2. Reinforced clay masonry.

Reinforced Masonry: Masonry units, reinforcing steel, grout and/or mortar combined to act together in resisting forces.

Return: Any surface turned back from the face of a principal surface.

Reveal: That portion of a jamb or recess which is visible from the face of a wall back to the frame placed between jambs.

Rowlock: A brick laid on its face edge so that the normal bedding area is visible in the wall face. Frequently spelled *rolok*.

SCR:[1] Structural Clay Research (trademark of the Structural Clay Products Research Foundation, a Division of the Structural Clay Products Institute).

"SCR brick":[1] Brick whose nominal dimensions are 2⅔ by 6 by 12 in.

"SCR insulated cavity wall":[1] Any cavity wall containing insulation which meets rigid criteria established by the Structural Clay Products Research Foundation.

"SCR masonry process":[1] A construction aid providing greater efficiency, better workmanship and increased production in masonry construction. It utilizes story poles, marked lines and adjustable scaffolding.

Shoved Joints: Vertical joints filled by shoving a brick against the next brick when it is being laid in a bed of mortar.

Slushed Joints: Vertical joints filled, after units are laid, by "throwing" mortar in with the edge of a trowel. (Generally, not recommended.)

Soffit: The underside of a beam, lintel or arch.

Solar Screen: A perforated wall used as a sunshade.

Soldier: A stretcher set on end with face showing on the wall surface.

Stack: Any structure or part thereof which contains a flue or flues for the discharge of gases.

Story Pole: A marked pole for measuring masonry coursing during construction.

Stretcher: A masonry unit laid with its greatest dimension horizontal and its face parallel to the wall face.

Stringing Mortar: The procedure of spreading enough mortar on a bed to lay several masonry units.

Struck Joint: Any mortar joint which has been finished with a trowel.

Temper: To moisten and mix clay, plaster or mortar to a proper consistency.

Tie: Any unit of material which connects masonry to masonry or other materials. See *Wall Tie*.

Tile, Structural Clay: Hollow masonry building

units composed of burned clay, shale, fire clay or mixtures thereof.

Facing Tile: Tile for exterior and interior masonry with exposed faces. See ASTM Specifications C 212 and C 126, and FTI Specifications.

Fireproofing Tile: Tile designed for protecting structural members against fire.

Floor Tile: Structural units for floor and roof slab construction. See ASTM Specifications C 57.

Furring Tile: Tile designed for lining the inside of exterior walls and carrying no superimposed loads.

Header Tile: Tile containing recesses for brick headers in masonry faced walls.

Load-Bearing Tile: Tile for use in masonry walls carrying superimposed loads. See ASTM Specifications C 34.

Non-Load-Bearing Tile: Tile designed for use in masonry walls carrying no superimposed loads. See ASTM Specifications C 56.

Partition Tile: Tile designed for use in interior partitions.

Solar Screen Tile: Tile manufactured for masonry screen construction.

Tooling: Compressing and shaping the face of a mortar joint with a special tool other than a trowel.

Toothing: Constructing the temporary end of a wall with the end stretcher of every alternate course projecting. Projecting units are *toothers.*

Tuck Pointing: The filling in with fresh mortar of cut-out or defective mortar joints in masonry.

Veneer: A single wythe of masonry for facing purposes, not structurally bonded.

Area Wall: 1. The masonry surrounding or partly surrounding an area. 2. The retaining wall around basement windows below grade.

Bearing Wall: One which supports a vertical load in addition to its own weight.

Cavity Wall: A wall built of masonry units arranged to provide a continuous air space 2 to 3 in. thick. Facing and backing wythes are connected with rigid metal ties. See *"SCR insulated cavity wall."*

Curtain Wall: A non-bearing wall. Built for the enclosure of a building, it is *not* supported at each story.

Fire Wall: Any wall which subdivides a building to resist the spread of fire and which extends continuously from the foundation through the roof.

Foundation Wall: That portion of a load-bearing wall below the level of the adjacent grade, or below first floor beams or joists.

Wall Tie: A bonder or metal piece which connects wythes of masonry to each other or to other materials.

Wall Tie, Cavity: A rigid, corrosive-resistant metal tie which bonds two wythes of a cavity wall. It is usually steel, 3/16 in. in diameter and formed in a "Z" shape or a rectangle.

Wall Tie, Veneer: A strip or piece of metal used to tie a facing veneer to the backing.

Weep Holes: Openings placed in mortar joints of facing material at the level of flashing, to permit the escape of moisture.

Wythe: 1. Each continuous vertical section of masonry one unit in thickness. 2. The thickness of masonry separating flues in a chimney. Also called *withe* or *tier.*